LUIGI

Gabrielle Ayers

Grosvenor House
Publishing Limited

This book is published by
Grosvenor House Publishing Ltd
Link House
140 The Broadway, Tolworth, Surrey, KT6 7HT.
www.grosvenorhousepublishing.co.uk

A CIP record for this book
is available from the British Library

ISBN 978-1-83975-090-8

Dedication

For all the Italian families who concealed Allied Prisoners of War and saved lives.

To Elizabeth,
With love
from
Gay x

Jim Ayers, who was known in Italy as 'Luigi'

Content

Preface

Luigi is a book about my late father who tragically died of polio when I was only six years old. In 2016 my husband and I made a pilgrimage to Italy to follow his epic trek through Italy in 1943 - 1944. We experienced an incredible series of events and reunions that were totally unplanned and unexpected. It is a story of exceptional emotion and joy. Seventy years later, to come across Italians who knew and loved my father before I was even born and who could tell me about him with tears in their eyes as they remembered him with such affection was overwhelming and an unexpected pleasure. Their families were so welcoming to me 'Luigi's daughter'. Luigi, the British soldier they had grown up hearing about. Luigi the Englishman who returned in 1949 with his fiancée to forge life-long friendships with the people who had saved his life. In 2016, our only aim was to pass through this village. To see where he had brought my mother all those years ago and to bring his story to life. This was not a planned reunion as we had no family name or address, just a few old black and white photographs of people proudly standing in a field beside a haystack; we could never have predicted what followed.

In addition to this, eighteen months later, after my mother's death in 2017 I discovered his entire collection of wartime letters written home to his parents over a period of almost five years, giving me a fresh insight into his gratitude to the families in Italy who had helped to save his life. Following his *Escapade in Italy* (his own account of his time in Italy) when he was missing presumed dead for nine long months, he writes home to tell his parents that he is safe and well and that 'it would make a grand story if someone could write it'.

This is his story entwined with ours.

Prologue

We are home.

But not from an ordinary holiday. It was something so much more. We are slowly gathering our thoughts and piecing together all that has happened. Together my husband and I have undertaken a journey that has turned our world upside down. It has changed our perception of life and questioned our beliefs. We have shared inexplicable events and we have shared profound emotion. It has brought us closer, if that can be possible and has had such an impact on us that we know we will never experience anything like it ever again.

That is what I wrote in February 2016 when we arrived home from Italy. I knew I had a duty to write an account to match my father's wartime memoirs that had inspired our trip. So much had happened that it needed to be recorded and as soon as I got home I started typing.

My father had died in 1959 when I was six years old.

I grew up with the scant knowledge that during the last war he had been a prisoner of war and 'escaped'. That he was, to his parents 'missing presumed dead' for almost a year and that he had 'walked the length of Italy'. I have since realised that some of these claims were rather exaggerated although undeniably based on fact.

I also knew he had been helped by two Italian farming families because he had taken my mother to meet them when they were engaged in 1949. My mother talked a lot about these two families. I knew that the Italian people had been kind to my father and took food to him when he was hiding from the Germans. She talked about Gino who was taken away to Padua for questioning. He was the eldest son and therefore the head of the family and that he had his front teeth knocked out with a rifle butt because he denied that he had been looking after two British prisoners of war. The other family lived in Comunanza and this was a place name that I heard over and over again.

It was all very patchy though, fragments that she remembered became like folklore to me. His story was part of my history and no matter how sketchy it was, it kept his memory alive.

After the war my father had written an account of his time in Italy and described it as something to hang his anecdotes on. It was, he says, never to be published for fear of retribution and for the fact that he had signed to the effect that he would not disclose any details of his escape, attempted escape, or anything of that nature. It was type-written and as a child I had read it a couple of times. I have to confess it did not seem particularly significant to me then. I remember that once he was in a straw hut and someone brought him food, or was it a cave, or was that something my mother had told me? It was all a jumbled story of things he wrote and things my mother had said and it all happened during 'the war'; that long, long time ago, long before I was born.

That long time ago was actually less than ten years.

And so it was that in 2016, over seventy years after the war had ended – and a lifetime to me, my husband and I decided to go to Italy, to follow his route and see it for ourselves. No-one could have predicted what happened. Whenever I tell people the story, whether it was to the Italians we met on our travels whilst we were still there, or to friends and family at home, I see their eyes well up and the goose bumps on their arms and I know they feel it too.

Emotion, incredulity and amazement.

The whole idea would never have taken off had it not been for my wonderful husband who loves driving almost as much as he loves me! He was prepared to make this pilgrimage with me and for me. He plotted a route, booked the hotels and a hire car and off we went. I can't thank him enough for his loving support because without him it just wouldn't have happened. I know I would have longed to visit the places my father had been and tread where my father had trod and see what he had seen – but would I have actually done it? I doubt it. My gratitude has no bounds.

He experienced this story with me and has become part of it.

There is no short version and once started I have to tell it all.

1

Jim

My Father, Philip Stuart Ayers, was born on 7 May 1918. It was to be the final year of the First World War and his father was serving in the army, stationed at Ascot in Berkshire. Their home was in Finchley, north London but his mother was able to afford lodgings in Ascot and wives who did this were known as camp followers. The baby was their first child. He was never called by his given names, except probably at school and on official documents, because to his family and friends he was always known as Jim. For some unknown reason his father Eddie was nicknamed Jim amongst his army pals, so when the baby boy was born he was naturally called 'Little Jim'.

After the war his father Eddie set up a business in Swiss Cottage selling antique furniture, ornaments and jewellery. The baby (Philip Stuart) continued to be called Jim and the name stuck for the rest of his life.

Seven years later he was joined by a brother Tony and despite their age difference they were very fond of each other. They all enjoyed a very happy family life together. His parents were natural entertainers and storytellers and his father was full of wise-cracks and witticisms. They loved life and laughed a lot; his mother was an accomplished pianist and sang at the drop of a hat. She liked Gracie Fields and I can remember her pulling out a large man's white handkerchief from the pocket of her apron to wave with, a la Gracie and singing 'Sing as You Go'. She was a lot like Gracie and I bet there was never a dull moment in that house. She loved playing cards and introduced me to Happy Families with the likes of Mr Bun the Baker and then to Old Maid. At Christmas we played Newmarket when the Queen of Clubs was referred to as Loose Lizzie; we played with real money, coppers mostly but as the evening wore on there were some sixpences and shillings and as it got closer to bedtime the odd half-crown would appear. Somehow it was engineered that I won all this cash and I would stagger up to bed with my new Christmas apron bulging with loose change. To me it was the perfect end to Christmas Day.

His mother had a brother Stuart and a sister Nell and his father had three brothers Arthur, Len, and Bertie (Herbert). They were all married mostly with children so there were many cousins to grow up with and family gatherings were always fun. He grew up like most young men, doing averagely well at school and with a particular interest in playing cricket and tennis. His ability to carry out maintenance and repairs was evident even then. He seemed to have a natural flair for it and was happy to take on 'Mother's little jobs'.

He had a special interest in the railway system and later as a prisoner of war was able to produce a pen and ink replica of the London Underground map from memory, just to pass the time. He left school and went on to Technical College where he graduated with a degree in rubber technology.

Gainful employment was the next thing on his mind though. It seems likely from a comment he made in a letter home during the war, that he may have worked first for a company called Andre's which made use of his degree in rubber technology, as he recalls the boiler there.

'Please thank Auntie Nell for her letter. She tells me all about selling the laundry (The Whittington) and a firm of rubber moulders taking over the premises. Are they going to use the old boiler or isn't the pressure great enough? Personally, if they are only a small firm, making small mechanicals as Dad said, instrument mountings for planes and cars etc. I should think it would do at a pinch. After all, at Andre's we only had an upright Cochrane. It was a bit larger maybe, and was oil automatically fuelled but then we did some quite large mouldings.'

His maternal grandfather was Harry Lay who started some of the first laundry businesses in London and when he died he left two laundries and several other properties. The Albany Laundry was left to his son Stuart and The Whittington Laundry to his daughter Nell. He left the other properties to my grandmother who once told my mother that during the war the houses were in the hands of an agent. The rents were controlled and the agent collected the money on her behalf. She said the properties didn't make much money and sometimes she owed them money. In particular they always seemed to need new dustbins which in those days were made of galvanised metal. She famously remarked 'I can keep a dustbin for 40 years, what do they do with them?'

Sadly, her brother Stuart was quite young when he died, but his widow Rene continued to run the laundry and it was Auntie Rene who gave my father a job as a trainee laundry manager at The Albany Laundry shortly before war broke out. This was a wonderful time for my father who enjoyed getting to grips with boilers and machinery to understand how they were put together and how to fix them when things went wrong. He loved the camaraderie of working with lots of people and was well liked there.

However, on 3 September 1939, war was declared. He was 21 and like thousands of young men he was called up a few months later and after a Christmas holiday at home he was posted to the Royal Signals Regiment and sent to Catterick in Yorkshire to do his basic training. That Christmas of 1939 was to be the last time he saw his family again until the autumn of 1944.

Once he had finished his basic training in the UK at Catterick he and his army pals were shipped to Egypt and at first he was stationed in the Signals Training School, in Nathanya, Palestine. I have a homemade photograph album of his time there and it shows how hard it was to take the war seriously when you weren't actually engaged in it! Every photograph in the album has a caption and his sense of humour shines out from every page. One picture is an official portrait and he is sporting a very toothy grin. Underneath he has written 'Have you Macleaned your teeth today?' Macleans was obviously his toothpaste of choice and I must have been brought up with it too, because seventy years later I am still using Macleans toothpaste twice a day! There is a picture of his bed with a mosquito net over it and it is in a dormitory with others, but this he says is 'the only place you can call you own'. The album begins: 'On Arrival, Abbassia Barracks, Cairo, Egypt, March 1940' where he spent his first leave. On 3 March pictures were taken of the Great Cheops Pyramid including one from the base and one from the top to prove he had made it up there and a visit to the Zoological Gardens and other places he had seen. Later that same month there are snaps of Tafiffa Barracks, Nathanya where they were able to walk to a beach and play cricket or bathe in the sea. It was all quite idyllic for them at times, that was when they weren't studying for their final trade tests or debugging their beds!

Once he passed his trade test, Signalman Ayers of The Royal Signals Regiment became part of the 22nd Guards Brigade who were responsible for all the troops in the Matruh area and saw front line action in the desert in Operation Crusader and later in the Battle of Gazala where on 20 June 1942 the brigade were forced to surrender at the fall of Tobruk as the city was besieged by Italian and German forces. Thousands of prisoners including my father were captured that day and in his notebook he wrote '20 June 1942 – In the Bag'.

Now he was a prisoner of war and along with hundreds of others he was put on a ship and taken to Italy. He was relieved to be out of the desert with its heat and flies and sandstorms and weathered the disruption to his life with a good grace, knowing that he was away from the dangers of the front line. He was moved three or four times to different camps before finally finding himself in a small working camp of fifty men at a village called Ponte San Nicolo, close to Padua. They worked on the fields as farm labourers during the day, which kept them fit and healthy. There were no restrictions on taking a shower and the food was acceptable. If things had not taken a dramatic turn he would have been quite happy to have spent the rest of his war years there.

It was whilst he was there in Ponte San Nicolo that Italy signed the Armistice with the Allied Forces. Suddenly the prisoners and the guards found themselves on the same side and Italy was in turmoil. The country was overrun by the Germans and allegedly 'there were Germans on all the roads'. Back at his camp they were told by the guards that they could do as they pleased. Either they could come back at night to sleep or to leave for good. After one night sleeping in the camp they decided that there was a real danger of the Germans arriving in the middle of the night, taking them by surprise and rounding them up, so they decided to split up and take their chances in hiding and on the run. My father teamed up with a 'Scottish Laddie' called Vic and they were together for the following nine months.

This is how he started his adventure which he later referred to as *'An Escapade in Italy'* and this was the written account I had grown up with. He had no way of contacting his family during this time and when he did eventually return home, he wrote up what had happened to him whilst he had been out of touch. This served not only as a record for himself but also as a background to the many anecdotes he had to tell them; they could understand better the trials and tribulations he had endured and how he had managed to survive; they could understand what he had experienced and his gratitude to the families in Italy who had saved his life.

It was because of this story that seventy years later my husband Brian and I decided to set off for Italy; just to get a feel of what it was like and to see the landscape for ourselves. We had been to Venice a couple of times for a day on a cruise-ship and spent a couple of days in Rome sight-seeing but apart from this neither of us had ever been to Italy. It was an adventure into the unknown. We decided to avoid motorways and only travel on rural and more scenic roads to relive his marathon walk.

My mother was 91 when we were making these plans but she couldn't remember the names of the people she had met in 1949. She said if you gave me a list of six names I might be able to pick out the right ones but she couldn't recall them for herself nearly seventy years later. She was pleased we wanted to go and looked forward to hearing all about it but that was about it. Due to her age and diminished hearing, her conversation was very limited at this time and apart from the old stories we had heard countless times before, she could offer nothing new to help us. We set off into the unknown backwaters of Italy with a few black and white snaps of people taken nearly seventy years ago (which had probably been enclosed in letters to my father after the war), a road map, a road atlas and a black and white picture of my father, taken during the war.

When my father started life in the army, nicknames were often given if something suggested itself. At the time Lew Ayres was a famous Hollywood film star, the second husband of Ginger Rogers and most famous for his lead role in the film *'All Quiet on the Western Front'* (1930). The lads were soon calling Jim Ayers 'Lew' (Ayres) and when finding himself in Italy a few years later the Italians called him Luigi.

It was only in recent years that Mum had quite incidentally mentioned that in Italy the families there called him Luigi. Thank goodness she did as it turned out to be a very important piece of information. Some years later when I had discovered all his wartime letters home I found that he explained to his parents that he was known in Italy by the Italian equivalent of his army nickname, Luigi.

2

Early Memories

My parents had been married for three years when I arrived on the scene. In that time they had modernised a semi-detached three bedroomed house from its almost Victorian state of neglect, to what I remember. Gaslight fittings had been stripped away and the house was rewired to include a light in the under stairs cupboard, something which my mother always thought was such a good idea of his. The dado rails were removed and panelled doors which we would now admire for their authenticity were replaced with smooth, flat ones which were the order of the day. I remember being with them when they chose the door furniture for the lounge and dining room. There were lots of door knobs and keyhole covers fixed to a painted board and they took a long time to decide on what they wanted. I remember that day particularly as it was getting dark and the very bright fluorescent shop lights were on. It was a brightness that gave everything a yellowish tinge. Maybe it was my first experience of such lighting as it is such a clear memory even now. My parents seemed to talk for ages to the man in the shop and it was all rather dull for little old me.

Every room at home was stripped of ageing wallpaper and Mum always said that she learnt a big lesson from this exercise as they would leave all the scrapings on the floor, night after night, with a view to sweeping it all up at once when they had finished. However, this became a mammoth task of its own as it stuck fast to the lino on the floor and had to be scraped off the floor having already been scraped off the walls. She soon learnt to sweep up and tidy as you go! Fresh light floral wallpaper replaced the old sticky varnished panels and it was 1950's chic! The kitchen and bathroom were improved and the back garden completely reconfigured. They had done it all themselves and were rightly proud of their home.

I have since found the condolence letter from Martin Fayers Ltd. Builders Merchants and Ironmongers and in it Martin Fayers himself writes to say: 'Knowing you and Jim from the 103 days in Hillingdon Way, I have always regard-ed you as friends rather than customers and have followed your activities in the house at Priory Road with considerable interest, admiring Jim's enthusiasm for the many jobs and appreciating your reception when I have called from time to time'. I guess my parents must have started the first 103 days of their married life at a rental property before moving into their very own home to start on this major renovation project. It was Martin Fayers shop that I remember visiting when my parents choose the door knobs over sixty years ago.

At home, I had the back bedroom and my parents had the front one with the bay window. The smaller third bedroom was my father's workshop and this was his glory hole. There were shelves all around the walls at head height jam-packed with bits and pieces and a workbench about four feet high which he stood at to mend and make things. He was very keen on making radio sets in old tobacco tins and I can remember the soldering iron and bits of wire. The headset had brown curly fabric cable and must have been just like he had used in the war. He always seemed to be wearing navy-blue all-in-one overalls and I guess this is what he felt most comfortable in at home and could undertake any job around the house at any time.

The story begins for me in my childhood memories of my father. Scraps of conversations overheard about Italy and bits and pieces belonging to him around the house; foreign letters with unusual stamps, his pipe rack, pencils sharpened with a penknife, an Italian/English dictionary, sepia postcards of Venice in a concertina strip.

He was the one I remember putting me to bed and the one I remember taking me to the bathroom in the night. He was my world and I spent a lot of time with him pottering about the garden, being in the workshop with him, singing together the two popular songs of the day by Perry Como; 'Catch a Falling Star' and 'Magic Moments'. We also sang 'How much is that Doggy in the Window?' which was another favourite of ours.

He belonged to the local Budgerigar Club and had built his own aviary at the top of the garden. (Many years later it was reincarnated to become a Wendy House.) I would be with him when he went in to see to the birds, to feed them and clean out the aviary and once, I remember, we had an egg in an incubator in the house; I wish I could remember what happened to it, but I can't.

I had a pet rabbit that I called Bunjamin (a corruption of Benjamin and Bunny Rabbit). He was velvety-smooth and silver grey in colour; he must have been the most compliant, cuddled and squashed animal that ever lived as I took him everywhere around the house tucked under my arm or he just hopped along behind me. He had a magnificent hutch that my father made for him and I loved that rabbit. I still have a picture of me when I was about three years old holding Bunjamin.

I remember checking Daddy's watch on a Sunday afternoon, waiting for the two hands to be in a straight line as I was collected at a quarter to three by Margaret who lived next door. She was only sixteen at the time but seemed like a grown-up to me and she was a Sunday School Teacher. We would walk up the road to the church and in a small side room with small seats and a table in the corner that boasted a small, rather smelly sandpit she would read us a Bible story.

One day my parents announced that we were going to get a car. It was a black Austin Seven and apparently my only question was: 'Will it have a back-seat for me?' I can remember walking up the running board as far as I could on the steep gradient as it went over the front wheel. Inside the car it smelled of leather and I loved it. The indicator for turning left often got stuck and it was my mother's job to reach out of the window and pull the orange flipper out. I don't know what happened to that car as we didn't seem to have it for very long. I know we continued to visit both Grandmothers by bus or train, which was our main form of transport.

One Saturday morning we walked together to the library. I remember the strong smell of floor polish and books and the hushed atmosphere. He chose a book for me and when we got home again I sat on his lap in a big chair in the front room where he started to read *Winnie-the-Pooh* to me. I think I must have fallen asleep after the long walk to the library and back as I don't remember anything else!

One of his old friends that I hadn't met before came to visit us one day and he had made me a swing. It wasn't just a seat with some ropes; it was a square seat with two bars on every side threaded through ropes on all four sides. It was painted bright yellow and red and was very glossy and smelt of new paint. I was very shy at that time and probably showed very little gratitude to this 'stranger' for such a wonderful new toy that he must have spent hours making for me. It was hung in the doorway of what was known as the lean-to and I continued to use it even when I could only sit on the top of the bars.

Another friend and his wife came to visit one evening. I was tucked up in bed fast asleep but in the dark my father came and got me. He proudly carried me downstairs to meet these total strangers. It was dark outside and the light in the front room seemed dazzling. I guess I was about three years old at the time. I did not want to wake up and I did not want to show them my pretty face, no matter how much they pleaded. I buried my face in my father's neck for the next hour or so, determined not to look at these strange people. I must have taken in more than I realised though because many years later when my father's wartime exploits became known to me I realised that I had been introduced to Vic and his wife. Victor had been Dad's companion during their nine months on the run in Italy. No wonder my father was so proud to show off his three-year-old daughter, getting her out of bed late at night, trying gently to cajole her into showing her face to them. Sadly she never did!

When I was five, my baby sister arrived on the scene and I remember my father taking me to the nursing home where Mummy was and lifting me up at the window to wave to her. She was sitting up in bed looking pretty and happy; it was June and a lovely hot summer's day.

My father's mother was known to me as Nana Ayers and her sister as Auntie Nell.

Auntie Nell had a holiday bungalow in Pevensey Bay; in the back garden there was a gate straight onto the shingle beach. Although it was referred to as a bungalow there was an additional bedroom and bathroom downstairs. The main part of the bungalow was built to be level with the beach but being so positioned on a slight incline there was a full flight of wooden stairs up to the front door which led into the rest of the accommodation, hence the downstairs space. The bungalow seemed to be only let out to family and extended family and there are some photographs of me and my parents having a holiday there before my sister was born.

It must have all been pre-arranged that when my mother had the baby I would be taken on holiday to the bungalow in Pevensey Bay by Nana and Auntie Nell. By now I was five years old and I have clear memories of it, especially of being asked to wear my red cardigan that zipped up at the front whenever I was allowed to go on the beach by myself. That way they could see me from quite a distance! I would go out looking for cuttlefish bones that were a treat for the budgerigars at home and any other pretty shells that I could collect. One evening we went to see Sandy Powell in a show at the end of Eastbourne Pier and another day we had Poly-Photos taken in Bobby's, a department store in Eastbourne. I still have those photos. They were happy days spent with those two elderly sisters.

Although unhappily, there was one occasion when Nana and Auntie Nell had an argument during lunch and Nana was crying. At five years old I was not sure how to deal with this as I had never seen an adult cry before and I found it very disturbing. I took myself off to the bathroom downstairs and hoped I could escape it all by locking myself in and refusing to come out. I must have eventually given in but they concluded that I must be very constipated to have been in there so long and I had freshly squeezed oranges at breakfast for the rest of the holiday!

My new baby sister was well and truly settled in when I got home a week later. I didn't mind and really rather liked her. As she grew bigger I helped to feed her as she sat up for tea with us in her highchair. She wasn't a placid baby as I had been. She was noisy, demanding, cheeky and altogether different. Dad apparently remarked to my mother: 'Don't think you've got another Gay there, because you haven't'. That was me – Gay short for Gabrielle. In those days Gay just meant happy and joyful!

The following June she was a year old. We had a family holiday booked for a fortnight at the bungalow in Pevensey Bay and preparations were made. One of the things I remember about this was Daddy making me a kite that we could fly on the beach. At his workbench he glued wooden struts to the kite shape cut out of brown paper. He passed it to me to paint but I can remember being very disappointed with my efforts. I was no artist but water colour paints from a tin of little squares on to the shiny side of brown paper just didn't work. Anyway I tried to do my best and feel some part of its creation. He told me that it would need a tail and that when we were there we could get some seaweed to attach to it or if that didn't work we could knot one or two of his white handkerchiefs to it. Sadly flying that kite was to be one of my last memories of our time together.

We travelled by train down to the coast and I remember the journey vividly because I had a new colouring book and pencil case for the journey. The pencil case was pale blue plastic and it opened up flat into three sections with elastic slots for all of the pencils, pencil sharpener and rubber. It had a new plastic smell that can still transport me to that day on the train and the excitement of going on holiday.

The middle Sunday morning about halfway through our time there Daddy and I went out to fly the kite on the beach. It was a breezy day and perfect for kite flying. I don't think it was much of a success though as I don't really remember a lot about it. I do remember that it was a very half-hearted attempt and we didn't have the usual jolly time that we normally did. Maybe it was because he was starting to feel unwell. It was as if I felt the storm clouds gathering overhead. It felt oddly different. As if he wasn't really with me.

I have since learnt that when we got back he told my mother he was going to walk into the village to find a doctor because he didn't feel well. She said she had never known him to be ill in all the ten years they had been together. He must have felt seriously ill or had inexplicable symptoms to consider it necessary to find a doctor on a Sunday morning. He did find a doctor and all I know is that he was told to go back to the bungalow and wait. He must have gone into the spare bedroom downstairs because I didn't properly see him again. At about 5 o'clock an old 1950s ambulance came. My very last memory was of him being carried on a stretcher out of the bungalow and down the flight of wooden stairs outside; a cherry red blanket covered him with a pair of wide black straps holding him securely in place. We watched from a bedroom window, Mummy holding the baby and me beside her. I can picture it as if it was yesterday.

It turned out to be polio and he was put in an iron lung in a hospital near Hastings. The following afternoon a lady from the bungalow next door came and sat with me on the veranda while I coloured in my new colouring book. My sister was having a nap in the cot and my mother went to visit him. I don't know if she got a taxi there or whether the husband of the lady taking care of me had a car and was able to drive her there. I only remember that I was upset that I didn't go with Mummy to visit Daddy in hospital that day. Only Mummy went and all my life I was jealous of the extra time she had spent with him that afternoon. I only found out about twenty years ago that she hadn't seen him at all that day or ever again. He couldn't bear the thought of my mother seeing him in an iron lung and refused her admittance. He asked the Matron to find out if his own mother had arrived yet and also if the baby was alright. Mum was crying as she told me that the last two things she told him were lies.

'Yes, your mother 's arrived and the baby is absolutely fine'.

He died the next day.

His mother had not arrived and the baby was not fine. My sister was feverish and stiff. We returned home to London in silence in a private taxi. Mum had my sister on her lap, swaddled in a blanket like a newborn.

Life would never be quite the same again. Mum was thirty-four and he had been the love of her life. My sister who at twelve months old had just started to find her feet and had started to walk around coffee tables or holding on to someone's hand, was now dealing with polio too, her right leg soon became visibly withered.

Once we were home again we seemed to be overrun with wonderfully kind relatives. Grandmothers, Aunties and Uncles visited often; they were kind and affectionate and I loved them very much, but they never referred to what had happened. More recently, I found out that my mother had not coped well with her overwhelming grief; it was such a shock and so sudden. The baby was sick and too young to know what was going on but I was six and I suppose everyone thought it would be best to put on a brave face, act normally and just carry on regardless. But nothing was normal anymore and it felt like it never would be. I had no one to confide in as even my mother was poorly in bed having succumbed to pneumonia and I felt quite alone in this sea of cheerful faces. No doubt they were all pitching in to look after us the best they could but it wasn't the same as before and it never would be again.

I hope children nowadays are encouraged to talk about their loss and their memories, but it wasn't like that then. In my presence at least, everyone kept up a cheerful and sunny disposition as if nothing had happened; at least that's how it felt to me. I knew that he had died and that I would never see him again and I found some random photographs of him (even cutting away the other people in the picture) and stuck them onto a single sheet of paper with sticky tape. It was a clumsily put together collection of five or six pictures but I hid it in my bedroom like some guilty secret, daring to look at it when no-one could see me and having a little and well controlled cry from time to time. A boy at school that I hardly knew asked me if I was rich now. I didn't see the connection at all. It seemed an odd thing to ask.

Certainly no-one asked me how I felt or started a conversation with me about the devastating tragedy that I was living through. I knew and understood that he had died and was never coming back but how does a six-year-old deal with that all by themselves? I decided that all I could do was to plead with God who lives up in the sky and that is what I did. I was alone in the garden and there was a blue sky with white fluffy clouds here and there. I looked up and earnestly promised God that I would always be a good girl and never be naughty if I could just see my daddy one more time. I was desperate and I cried a lot. I have clung to that promise all my life and I am still clinging to it now. I have done my best to be good although I am sure there have been times when I wasn't and I could or should have done something better or said something differently but I forever try to be good. I have never given up on that childhood promise.

You could call it Christian faith I suppose. I'm not much of a churchgoer these days, but the feeling is always there. Our Father who art in heaven and my father who is in heaven have become blurred into one and I sometimes have quite philosophical thoughts about it! God is all around each and every one of us but how does he manage it? Maybe our departed loved ones give God a helping hand to always be there for us. All my life I have felt my father's presence, aware that he is keeping an eye on me and smoothing my path through life. I guess I just couldn't let him go.

It was a cataclysmic time for all of us. Mum was thirty-four and mourning the loss of the love of her life. My baby sister had contracted polio and was to spend a lot of her childhood in Great Ormond Street Hospital as either an inpatient or an outpatient. It had affected her right leg from the waist down. It was her thin leg, the shorter leg, the leg that had a 'bink' (her word for her calliper, as she says that was the noise it made as she walked along). I was a very sensible and grown-up little six-year-old who adjusted to the situation we now found ourselves in. I was expected to carry on as if nothing had happened; to 'be a brave little girl for Mummy'. We became very close as I was her constant companion and always a willing little helper, in the house, in the garden and especially popping to the shops for things. In those days I could even buy her cigarettes for her. I paid the paper bill on a Saturday and did the weekly shop. I could go to the fish and chip shop and order quite a complicated list of three or four different preferences, which might include a skate wing for my grandmother, cod for mum, chicken for me and a saveloy for my sister, chips for four and I mustn't forget a couple of pickled gherkins! I enjoyed ironing and soon became as good as mum, taking over the job she hated. I could pick gooseberries, rhubarb and the windfall apples from the garden for mum to make desserts on Sundays; I could pick mint leaves and roll them on a board to make mint sauce with vinegar. On my seventh birthday I had a wind up alarm clock and after that I could get myself up, dressed and breakfasted. I had Weetabix with milk warmed in a saucepan on a gas ring which I lit with a revolver type attachment or failing that a match! Then I was off to school without waking mum or the 'baby'. Fiona continued to be called the baby, especially by our grandmother, until she was old enough to say very crossly one day: 'Don't keep calling me the baby, I'm not a baby'. As the years went by my maternal grandmother became a frequent houseguest, staying over the school holidays when mum had to go to work. I think she would have happily moved in for good so it was always a delicate matter for mum to find the right words to say that it was time for her to go home now!

Fiona had lots of hospital appointments to be taken to and Great Ormond Street Hospital, Out-Patients Department became our second home for a while. We lived in Hornsey in north London and from there it was a bus ride to Finsbury Park Station, a tube train ride to Russell Square and then a short walk to the hospital. Looking back I think I could have done that journey in my sleep! By the time I was twelve and at secondary school I sometimes went straight from school doing homework on the tube and meeting mum there. Fiona had a complicated operation on her leg when she was seven and mum spent every day with her. I would join them after school.

My sister's leg problems were a distraction that seemed to naturally follow-on from my father's death. In some ways it probably became a coping mechanism for us all as we had new problems to deal with, new places to go, new people to see, new stories to tell. As a vehicle it moved us on as nothing else could have and for us it was just how life was now. It was our new normal but I would never ever forget my daddy.

As a child one of the things that I learnt about my father was that during the war he had escaped from a prisoner of war camp. Having seen old black and white movies like *Colditz* I imagined it to be a very daring and exciting escape involving tunnelling out with much planning and preparation. When I found out that it wasn't a bit like that I was rather disappointed and it must have been around this time that I was first allowed to read his account of what happened and the places he remembered passing through; when he wrote it he had survived to tell the tale so it was just a record of events for selected friends and family to read and understand better what had happened to him when his letters had stopped and they didn't know whether he was dead or alive. It explained where he had been and what he had done to survive the nine months on the run. He called it *'An Escapade in Italy'*.

Every time I read it I seemed to gather something new that I hadn't remembered from before. It was typewritten and just something that surfaced from time to time. I was allowed to read it when I was old enough. Most of it went over my head. I remembered odd snatches of it but the stark reality that every day he was at risk of being caught by the Germans and worse still, that those who gave him shelter were themselves at risk of being shot and their farms being burnt to the ground did not register at all. I read and understood that they hid in caves and shepherd's huts and that people brought them food and I remember being told that they walked almost the entire length of Italy, but at the time it all seemed rather like a Boy Scout adventure and not a continual endurance test to somehow survive and live another day.

It wasn't meant to be a document of any substance or a historical record but with the passage of time it has grown to be more than he meant it to be. He writes in a cheerful matter of fact way but between the lines you can feel what it was really like for him. The uncertainty and lack of knowledge. The hunger and the cold. The fear and the loneliness. After the war when he was engaged to my mother he took her on a trip to Italy. It was 1949. As well as taking her on a romantic trip to Venice he took her to meet the two families who had helped him the most when he was on the run. One family were near Padua in Ponte San Nicolo and the other in a village further south called Comunanza. Comunanza was a well-known place name to me. As I grew up, I heard references to it all the time along with Gino from the other family.

Mum would often recall the plentiful food they enjoyed in Italy whilst at home they were still being rationed. Arrivederci was her cheeky word for Goodbye. She used to laugh at the memory of the girls on the farm. She had asked them what they did all day and she thought they had told her they spent the day 'Lingering in the Khasi'. It was much more likely they had meant 'Cleaning the Casa (house)' but the phrase tickled her sense of humour and she often said it!

She also remembered the life-size statues of horses on the roof-top of a building in Venice because when I had been to Venice for the first time she asked me if I had seen them; their trip to Venice explained the souvenir sepia postcards that I had remembered from my childhood. After the war my father had kept up a correspondence with these two families in Italy which explained the strange foreign letters that had arrived from time to time. They sent him photos of their families. My father may even have proudly sent photos of us to them; maybe a wedding picture or my sister and I as children. He kept up his wartime friendship and gratitude to these people who risked everything they held dear, determined that they should know how much he appreciated their help when his own survival depended on it. Their sanctuary, protection and support saved his life and he was never going to forget it.

More recently I've wondered if anyone had bothered to get in touch with the two Italian families to explain why his letters suddenly stopped. Did they know he had died? My mother found it hard to tell anyone of his death. Recently I found the one she had sent to Uncle Jack (who was later to become my step-father). Her letter was brief and to the point, written in June 1959 just days after his death.

Dear Jack,

I am writing to tell you that my Jim died last Tuesday, very suddenly while we were on holiday. It was polio.

I know you will forgive me for this brief note.

Sincerely Pat

She didn't speak Italian and our own lives were in such turmoil that I doubt anyone even thought of it. In recent years I have worried about it a lot. What must the Italians have thought? They must have wondered why his rambling and friendly letters stopped so suddenly without any explanation. It was so unlike him, so out of character. And for me, it seemed to be unfinished business.

3

Moving On

Time marches on and after eight years my mother re-married and we moved to Devon. My sister and I were nine and fourteen.

Mum had married Jack, an old friend of our father's. He and my father had met around 1939 at a Laundry Training School in Hendon, north London. My father was working for a family laundry in London and Uncle Jack (as he was first known to us) was also working at a family laundry business in Devon. They were both young men with common interests. They kept in touch, writing to each other during the war years and eventually both married and had two children each. My parents spent their first summer holiday with Jack and his family in Devon and bought them a bathroom cabinet as a parting gift, something I discovered was still in the house many years later.

Sadly, Uncle Jack's wife, who I had never met, died in 1963. He would sometimes call in and see us when he was in London. The Laundry Centre in Hendon had conferences and seminars and if he was attending one, he would visit us before heading back to Devon. I guess one thing led to another. I was happy and excited about this new development but shocked when I realised that we would have to move. We had always lived in the same house and it was our secure and loving home; the only home my sister and I had ever known. We didn't want to move. That house was a cocoon for 'just the three of us'. With no experience of change it was a very unsettling time.

All of our friends and relations lived in London, mostly north London. It was the centre of my universe and practically all that I knew of London, aside from Great Ormond Street Hospital and an annual visit to Selfridges at Christmas. There was a Moravian Church a few minutes walk up the road and I belonged first to the Sunday School, then the Brownies and later the Girl Guides. By the year we were moving I was fourteen and had been allowed to go to the Youth Club on a Tuesday night. I was very upset about moving and wasn't looking forward to it very much. When I mentioned to my friends at the Youth Club that I would be moving to Devon soon they referred to it as 'Dead Devon'. That really didn't help at all.

However our lives changed direction in August 1967 and it was a fresh start for us all.

As it happened I found myself living on the seafront road of a huge north Devon beach. Every day for the first year, I came home from school, and depending on the state of the tide, would change out of my uniform and cross the road to the beach and go hunting for shells. There were no cuttlefish bones but there were plenty of razor shells, limpets, mussels, cockles, whelks, and the bright orange scallop shells which were rare but were my favourites; I felt like I had found hidden treasure if I found an unbroken one. It was like being on holiday every day.

The first year I realised how mild the weather was in Devon as I had only worn my blazer to school for the entire winter. In London on school days I queued for a bus on freezing cold winter mornings, wearing a coat, scarf and gloves and covering my mouth if it was at all smoggy.

In Devon I liked my new school and found everyone wanted to know the new girl. I was invited to weekend outings and local events and I started to come out of my shy, sheltered London shell and began to grow up and enjoy life. I was now part of a proper family again with a mum and a dad, my sister and a step-brother and step-sister as well as the three crazy boxer dogs that were also part of our new family. I was happy and life couldn't have been more different. But my real father was not left behind in London. In my bedroom I had his writing desk to do my homework on and our old battered sofa which I slept on if I had a friend to stay over. These small items of furniture maintained a link with our old life for me. They came from our house in London and that meant a lot.

Surfing was becoming popular and I soon had a bodyboard. Encouraged by my new dad to go out with him every day when he got home from work, we kept up a surfing routine every day from the summer until November. I remember Mum standing on the beach in a fur coat holding towels for us. She thought we were absolutely barking mad. We didn't have wetsuits on, just bathing costumes but by November the sea was warmer than the outside temperature. It was only because we had a weekend away and missed two or three days that we were persuaded that enough was enough.

So the transition was not so bad for me in the end and although we never forgot about Dad Jim, and Mum would still talk about him sometimes, it was less so and seemed more distant as our London days faded into the past. Dad Jack was now Dad.

But for me Dad Jim was never completely forgotten, I still felt he was a part of me and the memories I had of him were still very clear and fresh.

4

Planning

My sister and I have married, had children, had jobs, become grandparents, but although we have settled in Devon, we still talk about our house in London, our schools, our old neighbours and our shared memories. We talk about her operations and her Great Ormond Street Hospital experiences. About family and friends we left behind and about our dad and the two families that he had taken our mum to meet in Italy, about Gino and Comunanza. It was our shared history.

My step-father died in 2004 and it was around the same time that I started to use the internet to research my family history; mostly on my mother's side at first. But eventually I found myself rereading my father's account of *'An Escapade in Italy'* and comparing his experiences with others I have read about. With the help of the internet I managed to find out more about British prisoners of war in Italy and read books by others who had similar experiences to my father. I wanted to understand a little of the political situation that led to his escape and eventually I even ordered a *Road Atlas of Italy* to look up the route he took as he walked down Italy following the place names he gave. I really tried to get under his skin and feel what he had been through and how he had coped.

However, a road atlas is all well and good, but as my husband pointed out that night every place name was on a different page. He came home the next day with a foldout map of Italy and spread it out on the kitchen counter. He asked me to read out the place names and with a pink and a green highlighter pen he plotted the route from north to south (green) and then the route when they had to turn back from south to north (pink). Now it seemed he was hooked as well. He even said we should go there. I'd always had this fantasy that one day I'd go to Italy and see the part of the country that my father wrote about. Now it was starting to take shape. The idea of going to Italy became something on the 'To Do List' rather than on the 'One Day Never List'!

I was fortunate to work part-time in a job-share arrangement with a colleague who happened to remind me that I could and should take a fortnight's holiday in February. Up until that year we had been having holidays abroad in February, but unusually we had nothing planned that year and I had started to think that I might find myself having a 'Staycation' at home!

My husband seized the bull by the horns. He suggested we plan a trip to Italy to drive the route we had plotted on the map. It wouldn't take the whole two weeks so we could even manage to have a week visiting the Amalfi Coast, Sorrento, Capri and Pompei while we were there; these were all places that we had wanted to visit one day.

And that was how it began.

It was about October or even November at the time and Christmas was the main thing on my mind. I was thinking about all the usual things like buying presents, decorating the house, planning the food, and going out for countless Christmas Dinners. There was no time to plan our trip to Italy. But then suddenly, it was January and the first few weeks ticked by. Were we really going to make this trip in February?

My husband is a Chartered Accountant and with the Tax Return Deadline being on 31 January it is always a busy time of year for him. Over the years I have learnt not to start any conversations in January that concern anything remotely stressful, like making holiday plans for example. However, when he raised the subject it was OK! He was worried like me, that we were running out of time. So, we spent a couple of Sundays pouring over maps and sitting in front of the computer looking at hotels and making decisions.

We decided to fly into Venice Airport (although not to visit Venice on this occasion) but to collect a hire car and head for Padua where the story begins. My father had been on foot and had been advised to avoid main roads as the Germans, who were occupying Italy at the time were everywhere. Brian worked out a route driving on the country roads with a manageable pace and where we would spend each night. There was a short return train ride to include in our itinerary and we booked two nights at one location to account for this.

We left home on Sunday 7 February 2016 to spend our first night at the Sheraton Skyline Hotel at Heathrow. It has an indoor pool area set up like a Caribbean resort and our first holiday snaps are of us sipping fancy cocktails at the (almost) swim-up bar and from the photos we took we could have been somewhere, anywhere, exotic! It was a great relaxing start and put us in a holiday mood. We were up early the next morning and storm Imogen was threatening bad weather. At home the gale-force wind caused some damage but she pushed us on our way to Venice, speeding up the journey and we completed the flight in one hour 25 minutes. After some difficulty in locating the car hire offices we eventually took ownership of our Opel Meriva. We studied the map and set off to hit the road. The car park was a bit of a maze and the exit signs weren't clear to us foreigners, but once we quite literally saw light at the end of a tunnel we knew we were on our way.

5

An Escapade in Italy

Dad's account begins like this:

In all that I tell you here I was accompanied by my friend Victor a Scottish laddie in the Royal Engineers.

We, 50 of us, were at a working camp, one of roughly 20 in the Padova (Padua) area at a little village called Ponte San Nicolo (St. Nicholas' Bridge). This is in the Venice Province about 30 miles from that city itself. The district is very flat with ditches, dykes and canals, something like Lincolnshire and the fens. Plane trees, rows of them, are also characteristic here.

I was amazed by how quickly we arrived in Ponte San Nicolo. As we turned into the main street we passed our hotel, the only one in town and continued down the busy road surveying all that we could. We eventually came to the bridge. It was a black iron construction and beyond it was a more rural outlook. The flat countryside was more evident and the buildings were old and in some cases derelict. One building in particular was quite large and I could imagine it once being the camp headquarters.

We found somewhere to have some lunch and I started on my quest to find out anything I could.

The restaurant manager was from Eastern Europe but he knew a bit about the town and was able to tell us that the top part of town (where the hotel was and the busy street) had mostly all been built since the war. Before the war it would have just been a country lane and fields with the odd farmhouse here and there. The original village was on the other side of the bridge where we had already noticed the derelict buildings.

After lunch and while it was still light we carried on looking around and stopping to take photos. I realised that I was only looking at old buildings and the countryside features; a derelict church, waterways and ditches, the flat countryside as Dad had written. Nothing else seemed relevant. There was a footbridge further up the river and Brian managed to find the way for us to walk over it and take more photos from this vantage point. We were really immersing ourselves in his account and only seeing the things that related to his experiences. It was as if we were airbrushing out anything modern or irrelevant to the story. We found the war memorial and took photos as it just seemed the right thing to do. We thought about finding an English speaker who could direct us to the local library and the pharmacy seemed a good place to start. The Pharmacist was only able to say in very broken English that it would be better to try in Padua. We weren't really sure what we could have looked for in the library anyway and decided that it was enough to actually be here in Ponte San Nicolo. It was the place where my father had been a prisoner of war and the first place he referred to in his account. I almost had to pinch myself to believe I was here and felt quite emotional.

Historical Information

On 3 September 1943 the Allies invaded the Italian
mainland; this invasion coincided with an armistice
made with the Italians on 8 September 1943 who then
re-entered the war on the Allied side. German troops
flooded in to occupy Italy and fought to resist the
Allied invasion. The Allies had landed in the south of
the country at the main ports, but it took nine months
before the Germans were in retreat.

*On the morning of 9 September 1943, we went to
work as usual. We heard the news of the Armistice
during the morning and 'downed tools'. The news
was later confirmed by our own British camp leader,
a full corporal. We went back to the camp and took it
easy fully expecting and awaiting the arrival of
Allied troops to take over. We had heard that the
Allies had landed at all large Italian ports including
Venice, Genoa and Naples. By the late morning of
10 September 1943 things weren't looking so rosy.
The guards were still hanging on though we were
free to roam about. The Sergeant in charge had only
asked us not to stray too far afield. Still later in the
morning an Italian Officer, dressed in civilian
clothing came from the Padova Headquarters at, as
he said, 'Considerable risk to himself' (erroneously
he thought that if the Germans caught him in
civilian clothes he would be shot). He had come to
warn us that German troops were on all the roads
and that we should leave the camp and hide during
the daytime in the fields, but return to sleep at night*

in the camp, or if we cared we could go for good but to keep off all roads. Actually, I suppose now, what he meant was that German troops were on all main roads and naturally if a prisoner walked down one of these in British Army clothing, he was sure to be taken. The impression I got was that every little road was unsafe and therefore Vic and myself and many others decided to lay doggo. (Actually 14 fellows left that day and never showed up again in the Padova area). Vic, myself and two others hid in a ditch all that afternoon about three quarters of a mile from the camp in fields strange to us. We talked to a farmer and on our return to the camp at dusk we met him again outside his house. He suggested we sleep under the portico of his farmhouse that night. To Vic and I this seemed safer than sleeping in the camp where if we were surprised in the night by Germans we would not even be able to make an attempt to break for it. We did this. Subsequently we stayed at this house being given food and civilian clothing undisturbed until 26 October 1943.

The hotel where we were staying was at the beginning of the main street and a good three-quarters of a mile from the bridge and old village at the far end of it. From our bedroom, which was at the front of the hotel overlooking the street, we could see that across the road there were older houses with fields beyond. I started to wonder if this could be the area where Dad and Vic had found themselves befriended by the farmer. Of course it could have been anywhere in that neighbourhood but for me it became a distinct possibility and it helped me to picture the story. To think he could have been here, just across the road or maybe even on this side of the road.

On 26 October 1943 six Italians in civilian clothing and carrying arms (rifles, revolvers or tommy guns), Fascists we were told later and all local people (i.e. Padovians) visited the house. We managed to escape as a child about 14 years old from the opposite house ran ahead of these Italians and gave us the warning. She believed they were Germans. We learnt afterwards, that pointing a revolver at the girl as she left our premises, the Fascists demanded of her what she was about.

She was frightened and said, 'Visiting this family'.

They then asked her, 'Are there two English prisoners there?'

She was scared and answered, 'Yes they are drawing water now'.

We had been drawing water for the cattle and got away with about a quarter of a minute's margin.

When we were not to be found in the house and finding no evidence of our being there in the manner of kit, clothing, etc. (with one exception mentioned later) these Fascists brutally treated the eldest son. By a stroke of luck this family had that morning dyed our British Army clothes navy blue and they were drying, hanging prominently over a wire fence in the yard through all of this search but were not noticed. These, otherwise, would have given us away. In Italian farming families the eldest son is the head of the household taking precedence over the father when the latter has passed about 60 years of age. They hit this son with rifle butts in front of his family, demanding he disclose our whereabouts. He stuck out that he had never had two English prisoners on his premises. He was taken away. To where, his family were not informed but left to guess the worst, prison camp in Germany or death. We learnt later that it was to the Fascist Headquarters in Padova, where he was subjected to a third degree treatment to confess but still he held out. They threatened him with all the tortures known to man but actually confined themselves to bludgeoning. There were ten Fascists and they worked in five pairs. They also tried to frighten him by threats of handing him over to the Germans and to shooting him, to all which he answered, 'If you do, it will be the wish of the Madonna!' In all this he even managed to tell them that they didn't get particu-larly thin on Fascism. They were all fat fellows! Eventually, about 9 p.m. in the evening he was made to sign a document to the effect that he had never had prisoners on his premises. He was told if he was ever caught after this with prisoners in his house they would shoot him and his family and then burn his farm down. After this he was released returning home very knocked about and ill.

A farm worker at this house, who lived some fields away, swore at revolver point that our suspected sleeping place, a truss of hay amid some old mattress covers in an old storeroom, was his own.

On this same day three other British prisoners, friends of ours from the same camp were taken in a house a little away from ours. As other prisoners were in nearby houses along this same road and the Fascists did not go to them, makes one suspect as spies, the occupants of the houses on either side of where Vic and I were staying, particularly as before the fall of the Fascist regime in July 1943 we were told they were active Fascists.

We returned cautiously to the house at dusk that same evening but before we reached it we were met by the elderly mother and later other members of the family, all weeping.

They were so frightened they wouldn't let us near the house and we learned that the eldest son and our three friends across the road had been carried off. We managed to get the remainder of our kit except that still drying, namely my greatcoat and our three Italian military blankets. There had also been a British travelling rug that mother had sent me but the Fascists had taken this. There was no distinctive marking on it, the sister of the house having torn off the Cash's name when she hid it with the others on her bed. The Fascists could not be sure but they didn't think it looked particularly Italian. We were given a little food and they pleaded with us to find somewhere else to live. Things seemed worse than they were. We imagined the Fascists would be everywhere after this and to move by daytime would be foolish. We decided to contact some of our friends and hold council. We made a big detour round our ground and cut across the road to a farm where one of these fellows lived. We enquired of the woman there who was outside the house and she said one of our friends was down the bottom of her field looking for the prisoner who stayed with her. All four of us joined up a short while later near a little shed made from bundles of maize sheaves, a tent like affair about 6 feet high called a 'cazzotto', in this field. That night we slept out in another field nearer the old camp with some more of our friends who had had news of the raid at our place. Such news spread like wildfire. They too considered it safer to sleep out that night. We got down to it under bundles of maize sheaves. By dawn next morning it was drizzling heavily, so the chaps who were furthest from the scene of the search returned to their respective houses. The remaining four of us decided it was best to get back into the dry of the cazzotto where we stayed all that day. Early on we were discovered by local people and before long all the families of the homes where the other two, Vic and myself had stayed and also where the three who had been living, all knew we were there. They brought or sent food and wine and told us that the Fascists had released their eldest son late the evening before. Vic and I had practically decided to move during the hours of darkness towards Yugoslavia. It was in the newspapers that Yugoslavian rebels were operating on the Italian side of their frontier and we thought we would stand a better chance of survival with them. However, calm followed the storm and all four of us decided to hang on. The other chaps were comfortably reinstated in their old farms.

However the owner of the cazzotto was still too frightened to let us stay on. It was near a footpath and there was a chance of a stray person overhearing us talking. The day following the rain, we were conducted by some other family to a wide ditch at the end of a field a short way from the house where our three friends were recaptured. We were told to wait there and during the day they would find us a new cazotto in which to sleep. By this time they had also arranged that our respective families, with whom we had each been living, would continue to feed us. This they did, by bringing it to the nearest house and someone there would bring it down to us. Our new cazotto was built in the farmyard of this same farm and to which we retired after dusk. This continued until Monday 8 November (i.e. about a fortnight). By this time we had news of a getaway scheme to take place near to the coast. The whole thing as far as we were concerned, (about 14 of us went from our district) was a flop. It did show us, however, how safe it was at this period to walk around in the daytime, to get food and a place to sleep, provided one took reasonable precautions and kept to farmhouses and away from towns and large villages. Vic and myself returned with some others from this escapade to Padova on 13 November and stayed two more nights at our original house, in spite of the threat the Fascists had given the owner. It was getting too cold to sleep out of doors by now.

That night, our first in Italy, in the village of Ponte San Nicolo we got ready for bed. I was in bed first and drifting off to sleep, Brian was still in the bathroom. Suddenly there was a very loud noise which I presumed was the television in the bedroom coming on with Italian being spoken. I assumed Brian had turned it on and would be holding the remote control in his hand. I waited for him to hurry up and adjust the volume as the din was deafening.

But Brian came out of the bathroom demanding to know what I was doing.

I had done nothing but then apparently, neither had he. The gibberish continued and the noise was embarrassingly loud. We hoped it was not disturbing anyone else in nearby bedrooms and frantically searched for the source of the disturbance. Was there a loudspeaker in the room for public messages? Was there a radio built into the headboard?

Eventually Brian remembered that he had packed a small transistor radio in his suitcase which was now under the bed. It had mysteriously come on at full volume and was perfectly tuned in to an Italian Radio Station. What was more, he could not turn it off. The controls were unresponsive. This was a radio that he uses every morning at home to listen to Radio 4 whilst shaving. He was very familiar with it and he had automatically packed it as part of his shaving kit! Eventually, the only way he managed to silence it was to take the cover off the back and remove the batteries and then peace was finally restored. We were stunned and very puzzled by this strange occurrence and couldn't understand how it could have happened. I thought about it for a bit but the only thing I could come up with, silly as it sounds, was that maybe my dad was trying to communicate with us, sending us some kind of message! I wanted to believe that he knew we were here and why we had come and that he was here too. What's more it seemed very important to me that Brian had experienced it first hand because if I had told him about something like this he wouldn't have believed me for a minute and would have tried to explain it away with a logical explanation. With this he just couldn't explain it. There was no logical explanation.

I have always felt my dad's presence and although it was almost 60 years ago that I looked up to the sky and promised to be good, I have always believed he was my guardian angel, always looking out for me, smoothing the way throughout my life. It seemed to me that this was his way of saying: 'I'm with you on this trip'. I remembered his tobacco tin radios and the coiled wire headsets and it all seemed to make sense. Radios were his thing and he was in the Royal Signals Regiment. Maybe this was his way of sending a signal to us. In the morning Brian re-assembled his radio putting the batteries back in place and it went on and off and on and off just as it always did. He couldn't understand it. I said to him: 'Say it *was* a message from my Dad, he wanted us both to get it. He wanted you to get the message just as much as me'.

I know it all sounds so crazy now but it happened and we have no other explanation. We kept trying to think of one but we just can't explain how a radio could come on all by itself, inside a suitcase tucked away under the bed, and also happened to be tuned in to a clear Italian speaking channel which then couldn't be silenced. It was the first time either of us had experienced anything like this and I could only put it down to my father's interest in radios. The journey we were about to make was in his memory and it was the only connection we could make.

We set off the next day with a feeling of being on a mission. What we were doing felt even more important now. Not just for us but for him as well. We felt he was with us whether we liked it or not! It was a strange feeling and as we got in the car and got ready to set off I could almost imagine that he was sitting quietly on the back seat. I actually looked back to check as the feeling was so strong!

As we left the village we passed through Padova on our way and I was surprised at how close it was, in fact Ponte San Nicolo was really just a suburb on the outskirts of the town.

We left on 15 November to walk to the front in an attempt to cross the line. We were originally accompanied by two Italian disbanded soldiers intent on returning home, both to the Allied side of the line. They proved 'poor fish' and were too frightened to go any further than the Ravenna area. The journey was practically uneventful except for many little minor incidents. The first lap between Padova and Ferrara was done on bicycles by the main roads, their owners coming with us this far to take them back. The remainder of our travelling was done on foot.

Our approximate route was Padova, Rovigo, Ferrara, Ravenna, Forli, Predappio, San Marino, Urbana, Cagli, Fabriano, Visso, Noccia, Amatrice, Campotasto, Grand Sasso d'Italia, Asergi, Barsciano.

We were heading for Rovigo and the landscape was still very flat with ditches and only trees breaking up the skyline. We imagined them cycling this part of their journey but wondering how the owners of the bicycles travelled if they were only there to take their bikes back! The countryside was all so open and flat. It must have been difficult to avoid detection and maybe they only cycled at night. We travelled on through Ferrara, Ravenna and on to Forli where we spent the second night.

A good friend of ours had asked if our trip would pass near to Forli as there is a war cemetery there. His mother's brother had been buried there but no-one had ever managed to visit his grave. We offered to find it and lay some flowers for Fred. The following morning we were able to fulfil this honour but not without some difficulty in finding the cemetery. It is on the outskirts of a quiet residential area and we knew we were close but couldn't find it. We were going over and over the same roads and eventually we pulled up to check our maps and instructions when we realised that there was a police car parked in the same road. It seemed like a miracle but there it was, parked up a few metres ahead. Brian sent me to ask them for directions. They did not speak English and I did not speak Italian but somehow I managed to get across that no, we did not need a hospital but we were looking for the war cemetery. I said the dates 1939–45 and that seemed to help. They spoke to each other for a minute and then asked if we had a car. I pointed to Brian at the wheel of our hire-car.

'You follow. We take you there!'

What wonderful chaps they were leading us at some speed through a no entry sign before bidding us a fond farewell with much handshaking and Muchas Grazias.

This is just an example of the moments in my life when I believe my Dad to be my guardian angel, always smoothing the way for me and helping me along when I'm stuck. Whilst we were at the cemetery we were able to understand some more of Italy's part in the war from the information boards put up for visitors which we found very useful.

From there we set off for Predappio and found the flat area of the north started to show signs of hills; mountains even. This day we encountered many hills and hair-pin bends. We tried to imagine Dad and Vic crossing this beautiful scenery with far more pressing worries than the next photo opportunity. Food and shelter for the night was all they were asking, but people were scared for their lives and not all were accommodating.

On the journey I was using my phone to take photos of the scenery and anything else of interest. I was also the official map reader and we were using the original road atlas of Italy that I had bought on the internet some years ago. It had a soft cover and was spiral bound. I had to hold it open with both hands and on one occasion whilst balancing a packet of biscuits, a tissue and my phone on my lap. We heard the phone make the shutter sound of taking a photo – twice. Brian was driving along but heard the familiar sound and asked me what I was taking pictures of. I showed him that I was holding the atlas open with both hands and said

I hadn't taken any pictures for at least 20 minutes. I managed to locate my phone under a biscuit packet and put the open atlas on the dash in front of me to look at the photos all prepared to delete a couple of fuzzy black specimens.

To my surprise there were two clear photographs of a village name sign. Molini. How they were taken I do not know and how they managed to be so crisp and clear I do not know. The place called Molini does not feature in Dad's memoirs, but we did start to wonder if maybe this was him communicating with us again. Was this a place he had been through, stayed at, or had some connection with? Was he saying we were on the right road and just because he didn't write the name down didn't mean he hadn't been here?

I want to say again that there must be a rational explanation for this second strange occurrence but as anyone with a smart phone knows, the screen goes to sleep; it goes black if it is not used for any length of time. One has to use a finger to call up the home screen, mine had to be swiped and then I had to touch the camera icon before I could even start to take a photograph. I just can't understand how these two photos were taken in clear focus, driving along at about 40 mph, from my lap while both my hands were holding the road atlas. After the strange radio 'message' in the hotel bedroom we couldn't help feeling that this was something similar. We didn't want to believe it, but it was odd and made no sense. It was much later when we were back home again that I remembered my Dad had a Box Brownie camera which he held at waist level to take the pictures. My phone was on my lap at waist level. Could my dad have had a hand in taking these photos? These two incidents were almost like modern day miracles. They weren't possible but they happened.

As a regular crossword fiend it has struck me that Molini is almost an anagram of the word million. It is just one L short of a million! Is this an example of my father's sense of humour? In the Italian milione (million) it is just one E short. It's one EL of a coincidence and he did like a joke! Another explanation in this vein is the Italian expression for 'many thanks' which are 'grazie mille' and which I always think of as a million thanks. Maybe this was his way of thanking us for making this special journey on his behalf. Whatever I think, these two photographs will forever remain a mystery to us.

We made a small detour from Dad's route to visit Rimini for lunch. It was February and the jet-set resort was looking a little shabby in the winter sunshine.

Most places were closed but we found a lovely restaurant near to the beach and enjoyed some respite from our dedicated cause of following Dad's route.

Back on the road we set off for San Marino which was next and we found it without too much trouble. The only problem was we couldn't find the road through it and out the other side. It is a very historic place set on the top of a hill. It looks like it had been a fortress in ancient times, very scenic and probably a big tourist attraction. As you drive up the hillside many roads lead to car parks. We wasted some time going round this place and I started to wonder if it was the wrong San Marino and that Dad was getting as frustrated as we were, as everything had gone so smoothly until now. There are several San Marino's in the country and maybe this wasn't the right one. It didn't seem the kind of place that they would seek sanctuary at that time; in Dad's words 'Too Palatial'!

I digress here to tell you our 'modus operandi' for finding a place to sleep and eat during our walk down Central Italy. We would wait until about half an hour before sunset and then select a farmhouse not too near a village, reasonably large if possible, not a palatial affair but having plenty of straw stacks near the yard. By this selection we usually found what we wanted, namely a fairly large farming family well off for food. Fascists and Fascist sympathisers didn't as a rule live in the country districts, unless it was in a palatial house. Having chosen our house we would hope to find to find somebody 'mucking out' the cattle shed on our arrival. This obviated the need of walking into the building to find someone to ask. There were not always kitchen doors on the ground level at which to knock. Most farmhouses are built with the kitchen and bedrooms above the cattle-sheds, pig-sty's and general farm storerooms. In any case you might try any of six doors before you found the right one. They are all alike. Having found somebody we would ask for the boss of the house (i.e. the eldest son or father or anyone with authority). Our question to him would be

'Have you a place in the cattle-shed where we can sleep tonight? We are two English prisoners'.

Sometimes the answer came directly

'Yes' or 'No' but more often it was

'Wait a bit'.

Then 'Come into the house and have a warm'.

We would sit by the fire and answer a few questions such as from where we had come, married or single, where we were going, where we lived at home etc. Later supper would be dished out onto the table. It was usually being prepared while we were waiting and cooking on the fire in front of us. Then we were told to 'Come and eat'.

Wine was usually provided as well. After another chat by the fire

'Do you want to go to sleep now?' would come and we answered

'As you please'.

So we would find a bed of straw and sometimes a blanket, old coats or covers of some sort provided. Never a word would be spoken before about being willing to shelter us. Of course it was not always as easy as this. There were nights when we had to ask at as many as seven houses and others where we only got a cold barn and no food. At one place when it came to going to the cattle-shed we went to the door of the kitchen and waited to be shown the way down. The woman said 'No, this way, you would prefer a bed' and promptly led the way to a bedroom with a real bed from which she removed the bed warmer of hot ashes. Then she left us. We nearly fainted on the spot but instead jumped for joy, stripped completely and got into it. Vic slept solidly, he always did but it was so strange to me that I slept but fitfully.

We were always ready to leave as soon as were awakened in the mornings but more often than not we were asked to stay for breakfast. This was usually at about 9.30 a.m. so we would offer to help while we waited. This was normally declined and we would sit round the fire and wait. When we were leaving we would be given a hunk of bread and sometimes a piece of cheese or salted ham as they said, 'Per la strada' (for the road).

Having eventually found the road out of San Marino going towards Urbino the scenery was amazing but very remote.

We travelled for miles without speaking for a while, both lost in our thoughts. It was starting to get dark and suddenly we passed an old derelict farmhouse after a long drive over the mountains. I got quite emotional as I imagined Dad and Vic walking for miles and miles and then eventually coming across a single farmhouse in the hope that the family would be friendly and offer them food and somewhere to sleep and then the disappointment they must have felt if they were turned away. It could be another seven- or eight-mile trek in that wild and remote countryside with the temperatures dropping as the night drew in. I confess to shedding a few tears. I really felt like I was in his shoes at that moment. We continued on through countless tunnels and various roads past Urbino, Cagli and onto Fabriano where we spent our third night. We slept well and made an early start for Comunanza.

Here I digress to explain that Dad and Vic had had walked down as far as Barsciano before turning back. As we were making our journey in one direction we made a stab at touching on some of the return places they passed so that we did not have to double back on ourselves.

Comunanza was in fact the last place they stayed and where they spent the most time at the end of their journey. It was the place I was most excited about visiting and where Dad had made life-long friends with the farming family there who had given them shelter. We decided not to stop for lunch or anything else and just press on until we got there. There was a heightened sense of anticipation because I had heard this place name mentioned so many times in my life and now we were almost there. Unfortunately Mum could not remember the surname of the family and did not know their address and as we were making the journey sixty-seven years after her visit in 1949 we did not expect to find out much but just wanted to be able to tell her we had been there.

About a mile outside Comunanza we came to a place where we had to give way to passing traffic to take the turning for Comunanza. We had to wait to let cars go by before we could cross. The road was angled so that we were almost parallel to the other road, we both looked to our right and there were three cars coming towards us, one silver, one red, and one dark grey; they were evenly spaced and going at the same speed. We took our eyes off them for a split second to check in the opposite direction. There was nothing coming so we only had to let those three cars pass and then we could pull out. We waited for them to go by. First the silver then the red and then … nothing. We both did a double take and checked the road. It was clear. Brian looked at me and I looked at him.

'I thought there were three cars?' I said, 'I definitely saw three cars, one silver, one red and one dark grey'.

Brian agreed that he had seen three cars as well. We were in shock. There was nowhere for the last car to go, no turn-ings off, no driveways. It had just vanished into thin air. It was the oddest thing and again there was no explanation. We had both seen the three cars but only two passed us. We didn't have time to dwell on it for very long as we were so close to Comunanza and we were keen to get there, but the following day when we were leaving Comunanza we reach-ed the same junction. Brian looked at me as we approached and said: 'This is that junction!'

We slowed down to see if there was any traffic on the main road before we pulled out and from the left a solitary dark grey car sped past.

'And there is a dark grey car,' I said!

Well we can't explain this one either. It is just something inexplicable that happened to us. Make of it what you will.

I know that it was probably just pure coincidence that a dark grey car happened to pass by us the following morning and had nothing to do with the disappearing car of the previous day but by now we were getting used to the idea that Dad was with us, having a bit of fun and making his presence known.

Brian was not keen for me to share this story because he felt it reflected badly on his driving and observational skills but I can't agree. It was a straight road in the country with no turnings off or anywhere for a car to go, especially at the speed they were travelling and they were almost upon us anyway. We took our eyes off them to check the opposite direction and waited to count off the one, two, three cars, as they went past so that we could pull out. We'll never know what happened but by the following day I wondered if we had been in some strange time-warp.

We can't explain what we saw but by now we couldn't help but make the link with my Dad; it was as if he was desperately trying to make his presence known to us. We will never really know for sure what happened. We tried to laugh it off and not take any of it too seriously but if he was communicating with us, maybe he just wanted to express his excitement that we were so near to Comunanza. If so, yet again it was something he wanted us both to experience. It was slightly unsettling but we were so wrapped up in the journey that we didn't really have time to dwell on it.

We arrived at the hotel and checked in at two o'clock. The owner manager was called Peppe and spoke a little English. As we hadn't stopped for lunch he offered to cook us omelettes and chips, even though his lunch service was officially over. While Brian was signing in I asked him if he was local to Comunanza and explained the reason for our visit. He was local and he showed an interest in some old black and white photos that Brian had photo-copied onto a sheet of A4 paper. These were the family snaps that must have been sent to my father after the war. He said he'd show them around while we ate our lunch but he didn't hold out much hope and saying with a wave of his hand clutching the sheet of paper, it's nearly seventy years ago! After lunch he called us over. He was with an older lady who was obviously an employee. She said she recognised a small girl in one photo who was standing with her father and mother.

'That was Roseanna Cozzi. I went to school with her. Her father isn't alive any more; but her mother is still alive and lives with her. They live in Rome now'.

Apparently the farmhouse in Comunanza where they used to live wasn't there any more but she could describe where it had been.

'Right,' said Peppe, 'I'll take you there'. He insisted on driving us and off we went.

'*The house we stayed at was about half a mile out of the village about 50 feet directly above the main road.*'

Instead of the old farmhouse there is now a modern Leisure Centre with lots of outdoor tennis courts but otherwise the position was exactly as he had described. It is not the main road that is directly below the buildings now but there is a road. In the course of the seventy years since my father had stayed here the main road has been constructed slightly below the site of this sports complex. It was a strange feeling being at the very place we had been hoping to find when we had only been in the town about an hour. I felt quite overwhelmed to be here in Comunanza at the very spot where my father had been. The place which he said had proved to be his salvation.

Peppe took us back to the hotel and chatted as we drove. He suggested that we could try asking at the Town Hall to see if there were any photos or information regarding the war years. He even drove on past the hotel to point out where the Town Hall was although it was easy to spot with its flags outside. Having thanked him for making our dreams come true he returned us to the hotel where we set off on foot to the Town Hall to make some enquiries. The young receptionist didn't speak English and pointed to a door. Brian knocked and opened it to find a seminar was in progress. A man and another younger girl came out and stood in the hallway to talk to us. The girl spoke very good English and the conversation concluded with them taking our email address and offering to get in touch if they could find anything useful or relevant. There wasn't much they could do there and then and we accepted that it was probably a dead end. The man was an official at the Town Hall and was called Domenico.

We walked back to the hotel to get our car and then drove back on our own to the site of the Sports Complex where the farmhouse had been to take some photographs of the land-scape with the hillside behind and snow-capped mountains in the far distance. It was all very emotional and eventually we drove away into the town. As we drove round the block, at the back of the hotel we noticed two ladies getting into a dark blue Jaguar car. I think we noticed it because it was unusual to see a British car like that on our travels so far. We continued on our way to go back round the town again. By now Brian realised that the Jag was following us. He slowed down to allow these local people to get on their way and not be hampered by us, the slow tourists! They didn't pass but slowed down as well. Then Brian pulled over and stopped. The Jag also stopped and two ladies got out of their car and came over to the window of our car. We thought we were in for a dose of Italian road rage! Maybe we'd missed a one-way road sign, maybe it was something else. Brian wound down the window slowly and cautiously.

'Are you English staying at the hotel?' We nodded slowly.

'Are you looking for family Cozzi?' Oh my God. What's going on?

We nod again. We're not quite sure why this exchange is feeling so surreal but it is and we're mesmerized.

'You know Luigi?'

This was the name my father was called in Italy.

I couldn't breathe. I was trembling and the tears were rolling down my face.

'Yes,' I stared into these two strange faces, 'He was my Father'.

It was a whisper, I could barely get the words out.

'You must go back to the hotel. There are family members who want to meet you'.

It was about four o'clock now. We had only arrived in Comunanza at two o'clock. It felt like the world had shifted on its axis. What was happening? We were suddenly being swept along on a wave of insanity. Everything was happening so quickly. What had been just a fantasy was beginning to take shape in reality. We had come to Italy just to follow Dad's journey and had half-heartedly shown those old photos to Peppe. Now two strange ladies were peering at us in the car and they knew my Dad's Italian name.

Although I suppose we did somehow hope to fill in some of the gaps that Mum had forgotten and to have something to tell her about our visit I really hadn't given a thought as to how it would all unfold. After less than two hours in Comunanza, here we were on the main street having a conversation with two Italian ladies who knew of my father and who was known affectionately to them as Luigi.

I was trembling and tearful and my first thought was to go to our bedroom at the hotel and tidy myself up. Check my face … I must look a sight … fancy crying like that. Deep breaths. Get a grip!

The previous conversation echoed in my head. 'Luigi'. 'Family members who want to meet you'. They said Luigi. Luigi. Family … who want to meet me?

Thank goodness my mother had told me that Luigi was what he was called in Italy.

I never made it to our room. As we walked into the hotel so did the two ladies we had talked to. One of them turned out to be a friend who happened to speak very good English. Thank goodness for an interpreter. The other was Patrizia and she was ushering in another older lady as well. This other lady was Elisa and she remembered my father very well. She hugged me and I was crying because I couldn't believe I was with a living breathing person who had known my Dad when he was here in Italy all those years ago. She said he was a good man, a lovely, lovely, man. Very special.

She was only a little girl of about twelve at the time but she remembered him mending their shoes, even making them clogs from a piece of wood; him being around the farm help-ing out and coming back a few years later with his fiancée. She also remembered Vic who was known as Victorio to them. I was holding a picture of my father in his army uniform and she saw it and was crying, 'Oh Luigi, Luigi'.

She wanted to know if he was still alive. I had to break it to her that he had died in 1959. She cried again and said, 'Madonna' and gave me another very long hug.

As soon as anything was said I was crying again but at the same time managing to smile as well. Very soon after this another older lady arrived and this was Maria, she and Elisa were cousins but had grown up together on the farm. They said at the time there were 22 of them living there. Grandparents, parents, and all the children; there were three brothers who were married and brought their wives home to live on the farm and then eventually their children of which Elisa and Maria were two. They were fascinated by the old black and white photos I had brought and were looking and pointing at themselves and the others in the family.

'Nonni,' was their Grandmother.

Then what followed was a slow procession of relatives. Elisa had two daughters Aida and Paola who came along and Maria's daughter Anna-Rita with her husband and two children. Elisa's husband Leo arrived wearing a red beret. Peppe made coffee and everyone was talking. I was being introduced to all these people by name. I was still so over-come that I was tearful but smiling for the whole time. Then I noticed Domenico from the Town Hall was there. He wanted to present me with a gift from the town and solemnly gave me two very heavy books (I immediately thought of our flight home!). He also turned out to be Patrizia's husband! So meeting him at the Town Hall had not been such a dead end after all! Far from it in fact.

With the help of Alessia their English speaking friend, I tried to explain that apart from Elisa and Maria, we had all been born after the war so they did not know my father and yet they were all so keen to meet me, Luigi's daughter who had suddenly turned up out of the blue. Why?

They explained to me that they had heard stories about the times during the war when my father and Vic had stayed with the family at the farmhouse. That they had also kept his memory alive and in their words: 'Your history is our history'.

I was truly touched. To think I had grown up with stories of Comunanza and they had grown up with stories of Luigi and here we all were, together and united in a very special way.

I thanked them all for coming to meet us, for everything their family had done for my Dad. I said that they saved his life and in doing so the family had put their own lives at risk. I said if he was here now he would thank them all from the bottom of his heart. I also added that if not for them my sister and I would never have been born. They were all such lovely people and I was still shedding tears and being embraced when suddenly a shout went up; 'There's a journalist coming from Rome'.

So that was the final stage of this joyous reunion. A very nice journalist called Francesco arrived and Alessia continued to give her amazing translations so that he managed to get quite a comprehensive story which appeared in the paper *Libero* three days later on 14 February, Valentine's Day!

One of my new Italian friends commented on Facebook 'If this isn't love, what is?'

Photographs were taken and Facebook addresses exchanged and I thanked them all for coming and for missing the things they normally would have been doing. I hoped we hadn't delayed the youngsters with their homework! They would hear nothing of it and said it was history and they wouldn't have missed it for the world.

At that stage I hadn't really had time to digest everything that had happened but they were absolutely right. It was history and we were making history.

'But why did you leave it so long to come?' That was the next question!

It was hard to explain that only now in my sixties with my family all grown up and with the support of my wonderful husband, the time had just presented itself; that we just felt this was it. This was the time to go. We prepared ourselves for a trip that would follow my father's journey in all senses of the word. It wasn't mid-winter but there were still signs of recent snow in the mountains and it was easy to imagine him there. He was with us and cheered us on when we were on the right track; he also let us know when we weren't!

The family were in high spirits as we said our goodbyes and they left the hotel.

'You must come again soon and the next time we will have a big party and all the family in Rome will come too'.

By 6.30 p.m. the last Arrivederci had been said and we were left feeling quite shellshocked by what had just happened. Emotionally drained and amazed at the way things had turned out in the space of four and a half hours.

I know I will always remember Thursday 11 February 2016 as Comunanza Day.

I never did get to repair my tear-soaked face, it would have been pointless anyway as I continued to shed tears on and off all afternoon. My husband was as shocked as I was at this remarkable encounter and when I caught his eye he was looking tearful too! He did take some wonderful pictures of Maria and Elisa looking at our sheet of photos and seeing their own family gathered together in a field nearly 70 years ago.

Once back in our room I texted my sister and gave her the news and asked her to let Mum know that the family in Comunanza sent their love. At that moment I felt like saying 'Mission accomplished!' My sister received the message on her phone in a supermarket and replied that she was crying and everyone was looking at her!

Peppe from the hotel knew of Elisa and her husband Leo as they live in a flat immediately behind the hotel and he said he must see her almost every day, on her balcony, doing her chores. It really is a small world. When we checked in at his hotel he had no idea that his neighbours were going to be part of this crazy story. The next day as we left Comunanza we had a different CD playing in the car. I became aware of the song that came on as we drove away. Michael Jackson was singing these words

> *You are not alone*
> *I am here with you*
> *Never far apart*
> *Always in my heart*

That was all I needed to set me off again! More tears. The feeling that he was sending us messages to let us know he was with us was very strong and whether we liked it or not it kept happening.

We were now heading for Barsciano and although we found ourselves on a slightly different route to the one intended it was in the right direction with the same mountainous features along wiggly roads on the map; lovely snow-capped mountains with their peaks peeping out above the clouds. Barsciano was the furthest south that Dad and Vic got to on their walk down Italy before coming to the conclusion that the safest thing to do was to turn back. They had been hoping to cross the front line somewhere in the area and be reunited with British troops but it soon became clear that it was just too dangerous to attempt any kind of crossing and although they were only thirty miles away from the front line they just couldn't risk it. It was December and it was getting perilously cold at night. They turned round feeling very despondent. They didn't know how they were going to survive the winter at this point. We found the village to be as clustered as my father had said and drove through some very narrow streets with houses on both sides and no passing places. It reminded us of the quaint Devon fishing villages we are familiar with at home. We took some photos to depict that this place was the end of the road for Luigi and Vic.

This last (Barsciano) is near Aquila. Here we turned back after travelling 250 miles. We were about 30 miles from the front line and just on the fringe of German troop concentrations. We made this decision from a combination of reasons. The Allied Air Force for one were bombing trains regularly in this area and prisoners, both recaptured and new ones from the front were being massacred wholesale. Most were killed in locked wagons. We heard too many of these stories to discredit them as rumour or exaggeration. A somewhat similar fate awaited prisoners transported by road, for road traffic was attacked daily by canon firing fighter patrols. These latter incidents also gave the Germans a fine opportunity for shooting prisoners if they ran from the vehicle to take cover.

In this district, the most mountainous we had been in, there were no scattered farmsteads at which to ask for shelter. All the houses were clustered in the villages and it was almost impossible to find anyone in a village who was willing to give us shelter. They were all too scared, mostly of one another. Added to this villages were few and far between, 8 hours walk across huge hills in some cases. By this time, 15 December we turned back, the weather up in those mountains was bitterly cold at night and the locals expected heavy snow any day. We only had scanty clothing, jackets and no topcoats and it would have been madness to attempt sleeping out for more than one night under these conditions. Also we were told that crossing as it was then, a static front was unwise. They added that the Germans had trenches even across the mountains, believe this or not. We were advised to go back and find a place to hide up until our troops made an advance and the front would be more fluid.

Here they turned round and it was on this return journey that they eventually found themselves in the village of Comunanza the place he says which was to be their salvation. As I explained earlier Brian and I were making our journey in one direction and so had visited Comunanza on our way down Italy. It was in fact their final and most memorable stopping place, their stay lasting almost six months on and off.

Our route back was Barsciano, Asergi, Grand Sasso d'Italia, Campetosto, Amatrice, Arquata del Tronto, Monte Monico, Comunanza. We did not hurry on our road back, our spirits were at a low ebb and we were pretty dishevelled both as to boots and clothing. We didn't see how we were going to find a haven of rest when everyone was so jumpy. We asked at each place we stopped if they knew of a farm where two of us could work for our keep but no one wanted two extra mouths to feed and with winter on them they had no work to be done. We stayed about six days in a shepherd's hut way up in the mountains just below the Grand Sasso d'Italia which is the highest mountain in this range. Our abode about 9ft by 9 ft was 7,000 feet above sea level and often above the clouds. It was a stone affair and had a small chimney. We eked out a small supply of faggots to keep us warm. The shepherds would bring us a little food from the nearest village one and a half hours walk away. It was a rest, but the loneliness, fear of being stranded up there by the snow due any day now and the knowledge that German patrols searched these shepherd huts at irregular intervals compelled us to move. We stayed two nights and a day in Asergi while our host repaired Vic's boots as best he was able with pieces of leather too small and pieces of tin. My toes were poking out but he hadn't noticed them! We didn't like to point the fact out. He was that poor he only ate twice a day and was already keeping a Yugoslavian prisoner.

We stayed two nights at another village on the false scent of a place to stop but kept going after this until we eventually reached Comunanza, the village which proved to be our salvation on 28 December 1943. This is near Amandola and comes under Ascoli for administration. The local people said that the place was very safe and the whole village was anti-Fascist. German trucks passed through occasionally but they hardly ever stopped. We learnt that some other British prisoners were staying actually in the village and many in the outlying houses. I estimated there must have been two to three hundred in all. Most of the farmers in this district were fairly well off as it was a big grain producing area.

On New Year's Day the snow that we had been expecting for over a fortnight fell with a vengeance to the accompaniment of a strong north easterly wind. This settled, not counting drifts and driven snow to a depth of four feet. After a day of sunshine, snow followed on the third day and intermittently for another two or three days, bringing the final depth to about six feet. This all made things comparatively safe for us and we stayed unmolested until the snow was really beginning to clear in March when even hill tracks were passable.

Rumours of sudden Fascist searches which might come at any moment were so persistent and strong by March that we were compelled to heed them. Fascism was growing again vigorously now under German protection and Fascist Battalions were being employed to search for disbanded Italian soldiers and escaped prisoners of war. Earlier in the year, on various occasions, we had to evacuate ourselves for a day or two, together with the youngest son who was of military age, to various relations of this family into other districts out of the anticipated area of the search.

We left by going northwards and by staying and working as long as we were able, where we were able, until a scare arose in the particular area and we were asked to leave or took off on our own account, we passed many weeks. We usually left voluntarily if a search got nearer than two miles! We paid odd visits to our family in Comunanza and then left again. We used to creep in after dusk down the hillside behind our house avoiding the roads. In the end we had established a long line of farms where we were assured of food and in some cases a night's shelter, stretching north from Comunanza to Belforte (about 35 miles distant).On our first return to Comunanza we stayed for a night with our old family but on the following two visits they were too frightened and we had to leave the same nights. There were over 150 mixed Germans and Fascists training in the village on those two occasions. Three other prisoners who had lived at a farm next to ours and whom we had come to know very well stayed on through all this period of anxiety living in a well camouflaged cave that they had dug in the side of a break of the land up the hillside of their farmer's ground. It escaped all discovery and Fascists had been as near as five yards and walked over the top of it!

The 25 May found Vic and I returning to Comunanza for the fourth time. Since the beginning of May we had had a very thin time; every area we visited was full of Fascist troops and even our old friends would look away when we passed or go off into the house. It was cold shoulder everywhere. Giving aid to prisoners was too much of a responsibility now. The Fascists punished those caught with destruction of their home and sometimes death. During these 25 days of May we only slept invited in a cattle shed once. Often it was under the stars or stealing into a barn and many days we only ate dry bread. Our last hope was to return to Comunanza and try and impose ourselves on our friends of the cave to squeeze us in for a night or two while we got some sleep and if possible for our old farmstead to wash and repair our clothing and also to feed us. When we arrived we found to our surprise that Comunanza had settled down and was comparatively calm, all the Fascists had gone except 5 or 6 who worried no one. We put our proposition to the parties concerned and both said that we could stay sharing the cave indefinitely. We did this, with the other three, sunbathing and passing our time on the hillside as quietly as possible during the day and sleeping in the cave at night.

We had the news of the fall of Rome on 5 June, D day on the 6th and on the 7th local news that the Germans were retreating on our front and were going to move through our village. They travelled at night and held up during the daytime, asking for or looting food from farmhouses on or near the main roads. This made things hotter for us and so we left our cave every morning at dawn and kept to the woods and dells higher up on top of the hill. At night we would meet our respective families carrying food for us lower down after dark when the Germans were on the move. This carried on for ten days and nights. One day it rained and we stayed in the cave all day. Another time we slept a night on top of the hill in a dell.

The Germans were being outflanked by the Allies advance from Rome towards Perugia which was north-west of our position and by the end they were retreating quickly. Many Fascist stragglers were on foot and came through in disorganised groups by the road and the Germans were using all forms of transport much of it looted, including horse, mule and even oxen drawn carts and wagons. We heard afterwards that one German Captain actually went through astride a milking cow!

The section that follows was found later in my father's handwritten notes and adds a few more colourful details:-

'The first of the retreating Germans started to come through Comunanza and all that night we heard the *clip-clop of horses hoofs. Movement ceased during the daylight hours because allied aircraft kept coming over to strafe any of the Germans who had attempted it. The German evacuation continued for 10 nights; they had used every conceivable transport they could lay their hands on. Oxen carts were commandeered in large numbers, donkeys, mules, and the (laugh?) of our family was one German Officer who went through the village astride a cow of which was badly in need of being milked!*

The last Germans blew up the two small bridges on the main road and then for a day or two there was perfect quiet and then allied troops started coming through. First a motor cycle patrol of about 10 Italians working with the Allies and the next day 3 or 4 Jeeps with real British (English types) came through and we had our first contact with true freedom for two years almost to the day. 20 June.'

On the morning of 18 June the farmers told us that the last of the Germans had gone through the village the previous night. We wouldn't believe this because we expected some fighting to take place and we insisted on staying up on our hill. During the day the Italians came up again and told us it must be safe for us to come down because patriots were running about the village carrying rifles and getting out hidden motors and cycles some of which we had seen and mistaken for Fascists. Also the main road bridges were blown and one stray German truck had been trapped and the patriots had taken its occupants prisoner. We ventured forth after this and about two days later 24 Italian regular machine gunners on

motorcycles fighting with the 8th Army came through and in the afternoon nine British jeeps came through. They were all using the secondary roads. We had a chat with them for a minute but they could not stop. They advised us to wait a bit and then get to Ascoli where we would find a British Headquarters. We spent the rest of the time visiting all the Italian families we had met in and around Comunanza saying goodbye. We were now back in the house and once again sleeping in our bed. One afternoon the patriots killed a calf and had it roasted by various people in the village together with fried potatoes and wine and gave a banquet for all the POW's in the district. The village brass band provided music during and after the meal. By this time quite a bit of 8th Army transport was going forward by the side roads but they were all Italian Units.

Vic and I planned to leave on foot on 26 June and to hitchhike back to Ascoli on army returning transport. We had to be almost rude to our Italian family before they would let us leave. On the morning of the 26th by a stroke of luck we met a truck in Comunanza village going our way and driven by a British Tommy. He had been taking stores to the nine jeeps and was returning to Naples. We got a lift together with some other prisoners and some Italian civilians returning to their homes from which they had evacuated themselves. This took us to Ortona by nightfall and we stayed the night in a Church of Scotland Hut YMCA. The following day we were put on a train to a place down the line called Torrino del Sangro. Here we changed our civilian clothes for Army ones and were given a shower a good British

Army meal and then we were put on the train again for Naples. The number of Ex-POWs by now in our party was in the region of 200.

I reckoned we had walked during these 10 months some 600 miles but Vic says it's nearer to 1,000. In any case it was a long way in badly worn boots.

After Barsciano Brian and I headed for Pescara on the east coast and just a little north of Ortona. We checked into our hotel for two nights so that we could spend the next day doing the train journey that Dad had taken from Ortona to Torrino del Sangro.

Our hotel was in San Silvestro just above Pescara with distant views of the sea. The following day we took a taxi to Pescara Central Station and caught the train which took us to Ortona and on down the coast past Torrino del Sangro where Dad and Vic got off. We passed a very flat grassy area just outside the station and imagined this could well have been an Army Headquarters during the war. It would have been a very short walk indeed and the perfect spot for army tents to have set up a camp of sorts, with the transport links of the train station right beside them. It would have been here that Dad had his shower, clean clothes and a good army meal. We think he would have been returned by train back the way he had come through Ortona and possibly back to Pescara (where we started the journey) so that he could make the train crossing to Naples on the west coast. Pescara was a much bigger station with direct links to Naples. However, whatever his route he was dispatched to Naples where he would have been shipped back to good old Blighty!

Brian reckons we drove about a thousand kilometres on this part of the journey. However, we were going one way in a warm and cosy car, chocolate chip cookies if we felt hungry, a plentiful supply of bottled water and a room pre-booked at a hotel to look forward to at the end of each day. We took six days to cover what they had walked on and off for nine months. There was no comparison to the ordeal that Dad and Vic went through. But in spite of this we really tried to 'feel' it as they did and see the countryside as the harsh desolate place it could be.

We were glad it was February as there were no signs of a commercial or touristy modern Italy basking in warm sunshine. What we saw was an unchanged wintry landscape with derelict farmhouses and rustic villages. Snow-capped mountains that touched the clouds and in places sheer rock faces that could only have been walked around and not over.

It wasn't a holiday but a pilgrimage and something that we both felt we had to do. Together Brian and I experienced this journey with all of its emotions and strange happenings and together we felt sure that Dad was with us as well.

We have renewed his friendship with the Cozzi family in Comunanza and completed the circle. They had never forgotten him and now they know that he never forgot them either.

On the British Airways flight home we were given a packet containing a bread roll and an iced bun for our refreshment. I had the strangest feeling when I read that the bread roll contained ham and piccalilli. Just to round everything off I have to tell you that I have not had piccalilli since my father died. He used to have it with cold meat salads and would pick out the cauliflower bits for me! We think he continued to look after us as we made our way to Sorrento and sent us unseasonably good weather on the second week of our trip. On days when we wanted to take photos of Capri and the Amalfi Coast we had clear blue skies and unusually hot weather.

We felt truly blessed in every way.

Historical Information

Having looked into this historical time in Italy we have now realised that there were around 80,000 Allied prisoners of war being held in about 200 camps all across Italy.

The Italians under Mussolini had been supporting Germany and the camp guards were Italian. Communications were not as they are today and mixed messages and instructions were received at different camps atthe time of the Armistice, at which time the Italians switched allegiance to the Allies.

Some camps received instructions to keep the prisoners together and to 'Stay Put' and wait to be rescued by Allied troops. These were the unfortunate ones. They were not rescued by the Allies, but rounded up by the Germans who put them on trains or in trucks. What happened to them is one of the most devastating secrets of the war. As my father had heard for himself, the Allied Air Forces were bombing trains in Italy regularly and prisoners were being *massacred wholesale* (his words). Most were killed in locked wagons. Those prisoners transported by road were also killed by the Allies cannon fire. If they tried to escape they were shot by the Germans.

In their defence the Allies thought they were targeting German troop movements and had no idea that they were actually bombing Allied prisoners of war.

The prisoners who made a dash for it and disappeared into the Italian countryside were the ones who fared the best because despite the tough times they had to endure, many managed to survive and suffered little or no brutality.

Of the 80,000 – it has been estimated that only one in seven made it home.

A Postscript

Once we were home again my sister talked about the photograph album that my father had made during or after the war. She had it at her home and I had no memory of ever seeing it before. I was eagerly looking forward to looking through it especially after our eventful trip to Italy.

It was full of 'off duty' poses with funny captions in his handwriting. But on the last page something caught my eye. He had stuck in a postcard which had a poem on it. I gasped as I read 'Not Alone' and the words of the Michael Jackson song came back to me.

You Are Not Alone

You are not alone
I am here with you
Never far apart
Always in my heart

Not Alone

By Patience Strong

We do not travel a lonely road,
We do not walk alone.
We do not grope unguided
Through the dark and the unknown.
For unseen hands reach out to help us
As we struggle on.
Unseen friends surround us
When all human aid has gone.
When sorrows come and faith grows dim
And nothing seems worthwhile,

If only we could see beyond the veil
How we should smile,
To see the folly of our fears
Our doubts and our dismay.
When loved ones walk beside us
All along the winding way.

We hadn't travelled a lonely road as we were certain that he was with us.

We had felt his unseen hands guide us through the dark and the unknown and we never doubted that a loved one walked beside us on that *Escapade in Italy* that was his story entwined with ours.

I feel comforted that although he never met Brian in life he has been able to give us his blessing from afar. After all, it was Brian who made the trip a reality for me. It was Brian who was entrusted to share in the experiences of those weird and wonderful happenings. It means everything to us that the connection we seem to have had with Dad was shared and somehow made it all the more special.

6

Returning

Having had such a wonderful welcome from the family in Comunanza and the invitation to come back as soon as possible so that we could join them in a big family party, we thought we should go back the following October and take my sister Fiona as well.

Since we had left Comunanza in February there had been a massive earthquake centred around Norcia and later another one that had destroyed Amatrice. These earthquakes were in the same region as Comunanza, roughly 10 Kilometres as the crow flies. I remembered we drove through the outskirts of Norcia in February, as it had a high wall around it and given more time I would have liked to drive in and explore but on that trip we were on a mission and nothing diverted us from the task in hand.

We had not seen Amatrice when we were there because it was the day when we got slightly lost and took a different road to the one planned. The road was going in the same direction and it was quicker to keep going than to turn around, so we hadn't driven through Amatrice after all. When I saw the TV pictures it was awful. I was relieved that Comunanza was OK but very sad for the people that were affected. The villages, homes, and countryside we were seeing now had a vague familiarity. We felt solidarity with a country where we now knew people that we considered to be friends. They had felt the tremors and the aftershocks and it had shaken them. Although they knew they lived in an earthquake region, there had not been an earthquake since 1933 and many of them had never experienced one.

That October we had planned to go back for a long weekend. We would fly out to Ancona the nearest regional airport on a Friday morning and be at the hotel in Comunanza by lunchtime leaving again on Sunday morning. That week, after a lull of several months, on the Wednesday evening when I was starting to pack a suitcase I heard on the news that they had suffered another earthquake in that region. It was close and I wondered if we should still go. I phoned my sister and spoke to my husband but we were all looking forward to the trip. Everything was arranged and anyway, what were the chances of another earthquake now. Our friends in Comunanza were having to live through it all, and had no choice in the matter. We messaged them and they understood if we decided not to risk it. They told us of the constant tremors and the aftershocks but said they had not suffered any damage at all. We didn't want to let them down, in fact it almost made us more determined to go and to stand shoulder to shoulder with them at this unsettled time.

We arrived in Ancona Airport mid-morning and went to the desk to collect our hire car. The conversation automatically turned to the earthquake two days earlier. They pointed up to the ceiling and described how all the light fittings had been swaying about. It was scary they said but nothing was damaged. The airport was over 100 kilometres north of the Amatrice and Comunanza areas, but they had felt its power. We found our way to Comunanza and arrived at the hotel by lunchtime. Peppe was there to greet us and it was lovely to see his familiar face once again. He said the hotel was practically empty apart from us three. His mid-week trade mostly consisted of businessmen of one sort or another. The main Whirlpool factory is situated about a mile outside of the town and provides a lot of employment for the locals and spin-off trade for Peppe. Only the most essential business was being conducted as the earthquake had disrupted regular events and everyone had returned to their homes and families at such an uncertain and worrying time.

We were soon aware of the tremors as we took our bags to our rooms.

Having lived on the coastal road in north Devon with the Atlantic breakers crashing against the seawall opposite our home, I have felt the shudder as the bed or even sometimes the bath shook. These tremors or aftershocks that we were now experiencing really did not bother us particularly. Only to mention, if we had been in our separate rooms and not together, my sister and I might ask 'did you notice that one at half past twelve', or whenever it was that we had noticed one.

We had a lovely lunch and then took my sister out into the town to see all the places we had discovered in February and a few more that we hadn't. The weather was glorious; we always seem to be blessed with good weather when we need it. It was sunny and very warm but not hot. We took her up to the hillside where the farmhouse had stood and we showed her around the town. We found the church and even the library with the help of my sister's recent Italian lessons and wandered alongside the old riverside properties. She loved it all and could imagine living in such a place, immersing herself in the language and getting to know the locals. We stopped to chat, leaning on the wall at the edge of the river below us. We wondered how we would respond to two foreign strangers appearing at our door asking for food and somewhere safe to sleep if it happened to us now. I guess things were very different then. It was wartime and times were hard for everyone and loyalties in Italy were divided. British prisoners who were on the loose in Italy having escaped from the camps were generally respected and helped by the farming families in the countryside who paid little attention to the threats of the authorities.

We made our way back to the hotel to have a rest and to get ready for dinner. We had adjoining rooms and agreed to meet downstairs at seven o'clock. Peppe phoned us in our room at about a quarter to seven to say that there were some visitors for us and they were waiting in reception to see us. Fortunately, it was good timing as we were all ready and rushed down to see who was there. A throng of faces greeted us, some familiar to me and some new ones. Fiona had her first taste of their overwhelming love and affection. It is quite contagious and overwhelmingly lovely. They had brought along Patrizia's daughter Fiametta who, although only sixteen years old, was a language student who spoke amazingly good English (as well as French, Spanish and her native Italian). It turned out that at the age of fourteen she was keen to go to language school and has never regretted it since. She said her parents Domenico (from the Town Hall) and Patrizia (one of the faces at the car window) were delighted that she could make use of her education in helping us out over the weekend.

We were introduced to everyone who was there and tried hard to learn and remember their names and their relationships to each other. Fiona and I were keen to make a family tree so that we could retain all this new information. In Italy it is the custom for women to keep their full birth name even after marriage, so the Cozzi name had been passed down from the three adult brothers who were at the farm during the war, to their sons and daughters. However, when girls marry although they keep their own family name, the children take their father's family name.

The first thing Fiametta had to tell us was that Elisa had only come home from hospital six days earlier having had a brain tumour removed. Although she was still frail and recovering from surgery, she wanted to see us and it was arranged that we should go the following morning at ten o'clock. The next thing to tell us was that they were holding a party in our honour the following evening. We were to be ready to be collected at 8 o'clock. I asked how many people would be there and they said about twenty. Not too daunting!

The following morning was Saturday and there was a street market outside. Whilst we ate our breakfast, Brian thought he would go and buy a bunch of flowers for Elisa. I also had a white embroidered handkerchief that had been my mother's and I decided to take it to give to Elisa as well. We were collected at ten o'clock as arranged and walked round to the small block of flats behind the hotel. Elisa's husband Leo and their two daughters Aida and Paola were there and Fiametta to translate. It was a really special occasion. Elisa was sitting by a cosy log fire with a bandage around her head but otherwise as chatty and alert as I remembered her in February. Coffee and biscuits were on offer, but mostly we just reminisced. She recalled how Luigi had taught her to count from one to a hundred in English. She was obviously very fond of him and so pleased to be able to talk about the time that they spent with him; they told us more about when the German Officers came to look around. How they had prodded with bayonets the very haystack that Luigi and Vic were hiding in; how their family had casually invited the Germans to stay for a meal to show their hospitality and lack of fear. What a time they lived through. No wonder the story of the British prisoners that became as family to them was passed on to their children and grandchildren as family history.

We stayed about an hour, not wanting to tire Elisa too much. We had given her the flowers as we arrived but it was only as we were leaving that I passed her the pressed white handkerchief and said it was from my mother to her. She was deeply touched and a little tearful as we said our goodbyes.

It had also been arranged that some relatives would meet us later on in the afternoon to take us to the site of the old farmhouse and show us where Luigi and Vic had hidden.

Two of the cousins came, one with his wife and one with his sister. There was an awkward start to this get-together as Fiametta wasn't there but we managed to introduce each other with the odd words we knew such as sister (sorella), husband (marito) and so on. We showed them the old black and white photographs that we had of their family and they were very excited to see them and were pointing themselves out to us. One photo shows three lads on motorcycles. Alberto proudly identified himself as one of the three. These were the old snaps that I had grown up with at home and Mum just identified them as 'the Italians'. Now we were with them and it was incredible. I never imagined we would actually meet them and have our world and their world collide in such an amazing way. I still marvel at the way it happened. Those old black and white photos were just a bunch of pictures of complete strangers in a foreign land taken long before I was born, but they turned out to be the link that joined our families together again.

Eventually, we were joined by Fiametta and things became a bit easier then. It is only a short drive to the place where it all began, but this time we were taken to the very spot where the house had been, standing exactly where the house had stood. Alberto had drawn a plan of the house and as was traditional in Italy, the animals and farm machinery were housed on the ground floor and the family on the floor or even two floors above. They pointed out where the outbuildings had been and then they looked across to the hillside behind us. And that they said, was where the grotto was. There was a cave in the hillside but it was all overgrown now. It was impossible to see it but it had been the place where Dad and Vic had hidden when things got dangerous. The children at the time but who were now standing here beside us as seventy- and eighty-year-olds, were given the job of taking up food and drink to them. It was thought at the time that if any reconnaissance planes were overhead looking for unusual activity they wouldn't have taken any notice of children playing outside, even one with a basket.

Dad's account became very real to us as we tried to imagine how it had been for them; how far we had all come to arrive at this moment. I still have to pinch myself to believe we have found these people with our shared memories of Luigi. They also spoke that afternoon of meeting my mother. She was a Patricia to me but Patrizia to them. It was 1949 and I told them how she was amazed at how plentiful and varied the food was in Italy whist they were still being rationed at home. They pointed at their ring fingers as they remembered how Mum and Dad were engaged to be married at the time. I was born just four years later so I am starting to understand how all these memories were so fresh as I listened to them as a small child myself.

Strangely, the Italian family had been having the same thoughts as my sister and I. If two strangers came knocking at the door nowadays asking for food and a place to sleep, would they do what their grandparents had done all those years ago? Times have changed now, but maybe if we had been the adults all those years ago we would have done the same thing. The circumstances of the war and the knowledge they would have had, that many thousands of Allied soldiers who had been kept captive in Italian prison camps were now at liberty but at the same time fugitives from the German authorities, would have put a different complexion on things at that time. It was a unique set of circumstances and gave the Italians a way to show their dislike of the German occupation by defying their orders which was for the whole family to be shot and their property burnt to the ground if they were to be found helping prisoners of war. These were exceptional times and exceptional people who risked so much to help soldiers like Luigi and Vic.

Once back at the hotel we had some free time before being collected for the party.

Fiona and I decided we would like to have a better understanding of how all the people we had met were related to each other so we devised a simple questionnaire to give out at the party. Recently Fiona had started to learn the language with an app on her phone and with Peppe's help as well, especially for the photocopying we cobbled something together. It was to prove a valuable exercise as once back at home we could clearly see which of the three married sons (that my father knew during the war) were represented by their offspring, now with children and grandchildren of their own.

By eight o'clock that evening we were being warmly greeted by our new friends who drove us to a remote country house – probably once an old farmhouse – where we were treated to the most amazing sit-down meal of many courses. In the end there were closer to forty family members there and they had come from far and wide to meet with us,

Luigi's daughters, some making a fifty-kilometre journey to be there. It was quite an experience! Together Italians are loud and exuberant. Fiametta sat opposite us to help with translations but my sister could understand enough to hear her hush her mother, saying that the English are not used to it!

I had deliberated in England before we left about what I could take as a gift. It had to be something that could be packed easily and not too heavy; it didn't have to be expensive, just a gesture. I eventually bought two round boxes of Cadbury's Roses Chocolates. As luck would have it we were seated on two long tables so when the meal was almost over I plonked one down on each table and invited them to help themselves. They loved the gesture and clapped; they loved the chocolates more. I don't think they had ever seen them before as they examined each one in wonder! One youngster told me he was saving his English chocolate to give to his teacher.

They also had gifts for me and Fiona and we were given a mini individual coffee percolator each with a packet of Italian coffee to go with it. I stood up to thank everyone and made a little speech, I don't suppose many could understand it but I felt that they had all gathered in our honour and something had to be said.

It was late when the party broke up but despite the language barrier we had enjoyed such a wonderful evening of genuine warmth and affection that nothing else mattered. They returned us to the hotel and said that in the morning they would be back to take us to see a farmhouse that closely resembled their old family home.

Brian and I arranged with Fiona to meet at eight o'clock for breakfast as we would be packing up to leave after lunch. Brian and I set our alarm for seven o'clock and the following morning we had hit the snooze bar once or twice before we started to wake up and were talking in bed. Once I was properly awake I needed to use the bathroom. I didn't go immediately as we continued to talk. It was just before half past seven when it started.

The shutters at the windows were metal and they started to rattle noisily. This rattling just seemed to get louder and louder. The room was shaking and the noise was deafening. It reminded me of a tube train in London that would rattle through the station without stopping. There was a rushing sound and a wind that accompanies such a thing. Surprisingly Brian and I just stayed together on the bed. We had no 'fight or flight' instinct kick in. We just cuddled up and waited for it to be over. The room seemed safe enough. Most of the furniture was built-in and nothing fell over. Just the bed was shaking uncontrollably. Many jokes have been made since along the lines of 'Did the earth move for you?'

It was reported that the earthquake was 6.6 on the Richter scale and lasted for fifty-five seconds although some reports said ninety seconds. When it stopped I made my way to the bathroom with some urgency now! The light would not come on and a plastic beaker holding our toothbrushes was in the basin. Fortunately for us that was the extent of our earthquake damage. Every car alarm in the town was sounding off but they were slowly silenced as their owners deactivated them and everywhere seemed eerily quiet for a while. The power was restored after about ten minutes and soon after that the church bells started to toll.

We could hear Peppe outside in the backyard calling out: 'Meester Bri-an, Meester Bri-an, are you OK?'

We went over to the window to see him and to let him know that: 'Yes, we were OK!'

Brian asked him if the hotel was OK. He tipped back his head to see the roof and looked it from left to right.

'Yes, 'otel is OK'. That was his survey done and dusted and his report given. All was fine.

Fiona had been asleep when it all started. She found herself lying on her tummy and clutching at both sides of the bed as the quake took hold. She very sensibly thought the best thing was to get out of the room as soon as she possibly could and was downstairs within about five minutes keeping Peppe company until we appeared.

I had checked her room but as there was no response I guessed she was already down for breakfast. We had put on the television to see live reports of the damage and devastation of a massive earthquake that we had just lived through. A convent had been damaged and there were pictures of nuns being helped through the debris. It was awful to see and hard to grasp that it was the result of the earthquake that had just happened here in our room, only twenty minutes ago.

Downstairs we all exchanged our experiences and were thankful that we were all safe and sound. It had been announced from the church that the morning service would be held in the open air. People were reluctant to be inside a building and were extremely jumpy. Our friends arrived at ten o'clock. as arranged but said they would not be taking us to the farmhouse after all. It was all too dangerous at the moment. They were sorry to let us down but they were visibly shaken up and one lady had found broken china on her kitchen floor after the quake and they were extremely unsettled. We said our farewells, took some photos and parted with much hugging.

It transpired that Peppe took flowers to his mother's grave every Sunday morning. He had heard that we would be going out and planned to lock up the hotel for an hour or so. As our plans had now changed we were happy to wander into the town and found a very large open-air café to sit out in the late October sunshine sipping our cold drinks. There must have been twenty or thirty people outside sitting at the tables. Twice, whilst we were sitting there we were aware of aftershocks or small tremors. The entire clientele (except us!) stood up immediately. They did not move but just looked around as if they were waiting for worse to come. Only when they felt the danger had passed did they sit down again and resume their conversations. It was sad to see that people had become so jumpy and scared of what might happen, but they had lived through several bad earthquakes that year and probably knew of people who had been killed or injured, maybe some who had lost their homes or their businesses and all because of these quakes; so put into perspective, we could maybe understand their nervousness.

It was only a few hours later that we were back at Ancona Airport and making our way home. I asked Fiona if the trip had lived up to her expectations and she replied that it had more than exceeded them. She had experienced everything I had wanted her to and shared in the affection and warmth of these people. She had expanded her knowledge and interest in the Italian language to the point where she was signing up for Italian lessons once we were home and it was certainly a trip that none of us will ever forget, especially the earth-quake!

7

Finding the Letters

Our lovely Mum died on 29 November 2017 aged ninety-three. It was a sad time for all of us and the end of an era in many ways.

My sister and I phoned to make an appointment to register the death and they asked us to bring any documents we could find like birth certificate, marriage certificate, passport, driving licence and so on. The next day we scoured her house but were unable to find anything other than her old driving licence in a handbag, but that was all. It was odd and we even decided to check in the loft even though she would never have ventured up there for many years. Amongst all the clutter and a jaw dropping moment when we realised just how much was stored up there and that we would eventually be responsible for clearing out, we saw an old black metal deed box. I remembered that Mum used to keep it under her bed when we lived in London.

Amongst other things, inside it was a carrier bag containing some old letters and also the framed map of the London Underground system that our father had drawn from memory when he was a prisoner of war. We couldn't believe it when we realised the letters were sent from our father to his parents during the war. There was also a notebook of his wartime recollections with information that would have been censored in a letter home. I couldn't believe what we had found. Mum had never mentioned these letters in all the many times we talked about Dad. I really don't think she was aware she had them and certainly not of their significance. After he died she would have put his belongings away in this metal box under her bed and probably never looked at it ever again. The letters were to his family and written long before they met; it was his wartime memorabilia which he had kept, but it wasn't really relevant to her. He had told her everything that had happened to him and taken her to Italy to meet the families so reading his old letters probably didn't seem necessary but now here they were like a time capsule waiting to be discovered. Having already written about my father and our own *Escapade in Italy*, I couldn't believe what a treasure trove we had stumbled upon.

It seems he wrote on average once a week and the letters started in early 1940, continuing until late 1944. He had asked his mother to keep all his letters for him because they would act as an *aide memoir* years later when he returned home. This was a rare find of amazing proportions. Not only significant because of its sudden appearance at this stage in our lives but also after almost eighty years they are now a reflection of social history in World War Two. Some were written in ink, some were written in pencil; some were on very thin paper and they were all very fragile.

The letters were a representation of *his* war. He wrote home once a week and described his journey to Egypt, the Signals Training School in Palestine, life in the desert, and then as a POW he wrote from camps in Italy and finally his repatriation and freedom in Naples waiting for a boat to take him home nearly four years later.

There was also a large notebook written in pencil of his timeline on active service and of things he could never have written in a censored letter.

I took the letters home and decided that I would type them up and make some sense of the muddle in the carrier bag. I realised that this was no mean feat but following Mum's death at the end of 2017 I had decided to retire from my job and now had more time to devote to this massive task. I gave myself a target of typing one letter a day. Some days I typed two or three or even more and some days none at all. From 1 January 2018 I crossed off a day on a calendar for every letter I typed. Sometimes I was ahead and sometimes I fell behind but if I did, I caught up. It took me until the end of July to type up everything he had written.

Due to censorship the letters contain very little reference to the war itself but are full of references to the many friends and relations who wrote to him to keep his spirits up and to keep him abreast of news from home. My father was obviously a very orderly and efficient man as he was fastidious in his numbering and dating of letters sent and when received, insisting that his family do the same. In this way he could pin-point if a letter had been mislaid in the post (or as sometimes happened, lost at sea). When he first arrived in the Middle East there were several postal services available to him and he tried them all for speed and cost, weighing up the best service to use. Sometimes speed was more important than cost and at other times a more regular but cheaper plodding service would suffice.

He was very aware of good manners and went out of his way to ask his mother to thank by name all of the people who had written to him that week and who had enclosed a Postal Order for say 2/6d (half a crown!). He was embarrassed to receive them but very grateful all the same. He was a pipe-smoker and good tobacco was always a welcome gift. Chocolate was not desirable because of the heat but a good homemade cake in an airtight tin was heaven sent!

Having lost my father when I was six, I found myself getting to know him in a completely new adult way. It was like hearing him talk to me as I typed his words. It was a fascinating insight into his way of thinking, his hopes and fears, his sense of humour, his turn of phrase and his abiding geniality and optimism. Yes, of course he was putting on a brave face to his family back home but I think he was genuinely being himself most of the time; he had to keep within the constraints of censorship so he could not tell them as much as he would have liked to and he would have told them a lot more if he could. To write a weekly report about nothing in particular was something he found quite hard at times but he must have been a gregarious chap as he always came up with something; celebrity gossip, radio programmes and music of the day, the flora and fauna (mostly insects!) of his surroundings, what clothing and headgear was worn by the natives. The food was a major topic and so the trivia of his daily life became topics to write about.

There were about two hundred letters, maybe more, in a jumbled order and at first I started typing random letters from random years. It was like a lucky dip! One day in the desert, the next day a prisoner of war. Slowly I started to piece together his story and as the number of letters in the bag decreased I was able to sort them into some semblance of order and began typing in year groups. By the end I had a folder for 1940, 1941, 1942 until 20 June (when he was captured), July 1942– September 1943 as a prisoner of war and 1944 repatriation.

As well as the letters, I typed up his personal notes about his movements and misfortunes during 'his war'. This was much more gritty and frustrating as he seemed to be going round in circles quite literally on one particular day. Front line action can seem confusing and chaotic to the individual soldier I guess, but one has to have faith in one's superiors no matter what. Orders are orders.

I started looking back over letters written at times that I could now marry up with his actual movements at the corresponding time. It was quite bizarre but showed another side of him; the one where you can shut off from your present predicament in order to write a perfectly normal letter home, commenting on the state of the garden or the local railway service whilst mentally recovering from an overnight raid or shaking sand off the notepaper because a sandstorm was in progress.

It was all like a massive jigsaw puzzle but very rewarding to have the full picture by the end. There are some letters missing but I still consider it to be a complete picture.

It seemed that every spare minute I had I was engrossed in typing and reading his letters or looking up place names and events that he referred to. My husband was telling people that I had lost my mother but found my father.

As always he was not far wrong!

His first letter home from Naples was particularly poignant as he had been reported to his family as 'Missing. Presumed Dead' and they had received no news for almost a year. But it was also very encouraging for me to read, over seventy years later, that he could imagine his story becoming a book one day, 'if only someone could write it properly'

30.6.44

Somewhere near Naples

Italy

My Dear Mum, Dad and Tony,

Get busy feeding fatted calf! I expect you will be more overjoyed to receive good news of me than I am to be in this position to send it. It was two years all but 3 days.

I seem to be in good health – if my weight is any indication; for I weigh more now than on my calling-up. And I don't think I have any hidden complaints – I sincerely hope not.

I am still with Victor Gilchrist of Edinburgh whose wife you may have heard from. We have shared most of our exploits of the last 12 months together. **It would make a grand story if someone could write it properly with many a humoristic side to it. At least, on looking back, many events which at the time seemed serious business, we can now smile at.**

Incidentally, to put your minds at rest in case you have in the past imagined otherwise, I have never suffered any brutality, only hardships.

And I suppose you in turn are most keen to know when you will see 'yours sincerely' again. All I can say is 'before long' so get fattening up that calf – 'cos I'm raring to go!

My love to you all.

Your days of waiting for news have finished.

As always your loving Son and Brother

Jim

In January 2018 I was stunned to receive a *Messenger* message from a stranger in Italy. Someone called Emanuele had miraculously managed to find me through *Facebook*. Having done a search on the internet for his village name he had seen the newspaper article from 14.2.16 which mentioned that my father had been in a prisoner of war camp there. They had little of no knowledge of the camp and asked for my help.

14 January 2018

Dear Mrs Ross

My name is Emanuele, from Padova, Italy. I'm writing you because I am realizing an historic search on the WWII Prisoner Camp of Ponte San Nicolo (Padova) with the local municipality and the National Partisan Association of Italy. I know from local press that your father, Mr. Jim Ayers, has been in the Prisoner Camp in Ponte San Nicolo, from there he has escaped and then he has been hidden by Cozzi family in Comunanza (Ascoli Piceno). We have very few infos about the Prisoner Camp, no-one there have memory about, but for us it will be very helpful to be contacted. I kindly ask you to contact me by email. Many thanks for your help. Emanuele.

If there was ever a time I needed to be sent an angel this was it.

I was a mere few days into my new project but I had already stumbled across a letter my father had left with Gino in Ponte San Nicolo. This is the village where my father and Vic spent their first six weeks as escapees. The letter was left at the farmhouse with instructions that it should be handed to the first British soldier they met however long it took. It was a special letter that he wrote to his parents telling them about this courageous family in Ponte San Nicolo who had sheltered him and protected him in the first days of his freedom. They had risked their lives by doing so and Gino, the eldest son and head of the family, had been brutally beaten and questioned about the fact that there was reason to believe he was harbouring British prisoners, something Gino strenuously denied. He came home in a very bad way and with his front teeth knocked out. It was at this point that my father and Vic decided that they could not put this family at risk any longer and made plans to walk to the front line to be repatriated with the Allied Forces.

In the letter I'd typed, my father was asking his parents that should anything happen to him, they absolutely must recompense this family for all they had done. He spoke of the kindness and affection they had shown him. He told his parents how they had saved his life and nothing would be too good for them. He gave their address and family name as well as naming every one in the family even giving the children's ages.

He had left this letter with Gino to be sent home to England when the Allied Forces arrived. This highly incriminating document actually arrived in London twenty months later, by which time my father had returned home in person from his exploits in Italy! Where it was hidden in the farmhouse is a mystery, but it would surely have been their death warrant if it had ever been found.

8

The Farmhouse Letter

My father and his companion Vic spent the first six weeks of 'freedom' in the farmhouse less than a mile away from the prison camp. An amazing family looked after and sheltered them and treated them like their own sons. They were hidden but well fed, happy and at first secure.

They hoped they would be picked up by passing British troops but it soon became clear that there were no passing troops where they were in Padua. It was true that Allied troops were landing in the southern ports but they faced fierce fighting from the occupying German forces as they made their way north. It would be many months before the Allies reached their corner of Italy in Padua.

The Germans encouraged Italian Fascists to spy for them and it came to their attention that there could be British prisoners of war staying at the farmhouse.

When the head of the family was taken away for questioning, returning the next day in a very bad state, my father and Vic decided it was time to move on before they put this family in any more danger. Not knowing what the future held, my father wrote a letter to his parents in London, explaining how these people had saved his life and that nothing was too good for them. They left the letter with the family to be given to the first British soldier they met.

If ever a document could be more incriminating than this one I cannot imagine it!

Letter dated 28.10.43

Arrived June 1945

> Signor Marzotto Giuseppe
> Via Passoveggiani
> Salboro N.40
> Padua, Italia.

My Dear Mum, Dad and Tony,

I am writing this letter on the above date to be posted by the holder as soon as he is able, (i.e. after the arrival of the Allied Forces). Since we were released on 9 Sept. I have been staying with an Italian Country Family. Two days ago, however, the house was raided by Fascists who had information that we were there. Luckily we just got away in time but as the raiders could not find us or any definite evidence of our being there, they took away the boss of the house (the eldest son) and subjected him to 3rd degree treatment to confess but like a hero he said nothing and he was released. The Germans are doing little to find prisoners but leaving the spying and capture to the Fascists.

At present we are sleeping and staying away from any houses and are soon to attempt to join our forces or the Yugo-Slavian rebels. We have waited too long for our boys to reach us. I am leaving this letter in the hands of the family, whose address is at the top, and who have kept us these 6 weeks. I say we because this includes Victor Gilchrist who has been with me since the Italian Armistice.

This family who live only a short distance from my old working camp have treated us like their brothers and although food is scarce in this country we have never once gone hungry. They have given us civilian clothes and we have always had a bed. They look upon themselves as our saviours which is in fact what they are. Anything I can do for them after this, when I am able, will be done willingly but just in case I can't, I trust you will endeavour to compensate them for me. Also they may be able to give you valuable information as to my future happenings. At all events contact them and as they understand no English you will have to write in Italian. Their surname is Marzotto and they consist of a Grandfather Giuseppe, a Grandmother Albina, their two married sons Gino and Tony and an unmarried daughter Pasquina. Gino's wife is Gisira and Tony's Asenta. Gino has four children, a girl aged 14 Mafalda, a boy 12 Elio, a girl 10 Lucia and Guiseppe who is 6 months old. Tony has two. A boy 5 Rhino and a girl 3 called Angelina. They all send greetings to you. Incidentally, they know me best by the Italian equivalent to my army nickname Luigi.

They have taken grave risks in harbouring us and the whole family have been threatened with death if British are found there again, so I feel nothing is too good for them. At present we feel very much the hunted but hope things to be better soon. At least we have plenty to eat and drink. I weigh 10 stone 1 lb which is more than I ever did at home.

I have thought of you all much these days and hope you haven't worried too much in the absence of any news from me. News of our lads advance reaches us, London version, 2nd or 3rd hand and it seems today a very great advance has been made to near Florence. So there is plenty of hope yet.

Here is Victor's wife's address Mrs V. Gilchrist, 1 Spitalfields Crescent, Edinburgh.

I shall always be thinking of you and always hope to be with you soon. Remember me to all friends and relations.

As ever your loving son and brother.

Jim

Several weeks after setting out on foot to make their way south Luigi and Vic sent a postcard to their Italian family to let them know that so far they were safe and well. In order to avoid suspicion they pretended to be two girls using the feminine version of their names.

Postcard Addressed to

Sig Marzotto Guiseppe
Via Passeveggiano
Salboro No 40
Padova

8.12.43
Place sent from:-
Presci
Macerata
Caro Gino,
Dear Gino,
Vi scritto quesli cartolina, si troviamo noi due beni, sperriamo tu, & tutti in familgia
We are writing this card to say we are both well and hope you and the family

& bene
are good too.
Saluti & bacci tutti
Regards and kisses to you all
Vittoria and Luigina
Victoria and *Luigina*

When we had first visited Ponte San Nicolo in February 2016 we did not have any information to go on as I was only to find these letters nearly two years later. Now I miraculously had a contact in Ponte San Nicolo and I had all the details of the family. This family where my father was told he was like a son to them, where he had been so well looked after and loved by them and where he had taken my mother to meet them after the war. Although the family details were now over seventy years out of date I wondered if it would be enough information to trace them.

I replied to Emanuele very briefly at first; partly because we were genuinely snowed under with other domestic issues and partly to be cautious. I had only had the letters for a month and had barely scratched the surface of this mammoth task. I had read odd letters and had started to type them up but they were all so jumbled that to find any references to the camp at Ponte San Nicolo was like finding a needle in a haystack. I explained to him that following my mother's death we were still very busy but that I promised to get back to him as soon as I could.

When a few weeks later I replied to him, I was in a better position to give him the little information I had, but asked him if it was possible he could do something for me in return. I told him about the family who had lived and farmed in Ponte San Nicolo at the time of my father's release and who had taken pity on him and Vic, hiding them from the authorities at great risk to themselves. I was now able to give him the family name and wartime address. Emanuele said he would try and find out if there were any family members still in the area.

Over the next few months we exchanged brief messages, mostly to the effect that he had drawn a blank wherever he tried. To his credit, he decided to put a message on *Facebook*. I don't know the details but by the beginning of July he had some hopeful news and by the end of July he was in contact with someone. Apparently there were some family members who agreed to meet Emanuele to talk about the British Prisoner of War called Luigi. It was Lucia and Angelina, cousins who grew up together on the farm. They had been aged 10 and five in 1943. Now they were aged 80 and 85.

They laid on a great feast in his honour and like the Cozzi family in Comunanza were only too happy to reminisce about Luigi and how he had come back in 1949 with his fiancée. They had about ten black and white photos he had taken at that visit and Emanuele emailed copies of them to me. One snap of the elderly mother and father had written on the back 'Taken by English Soldier Luigi'. There was one particular photo of my parents which brought tears to my eyes as I had never seen it before and yet this Italian family had kept it safe after all these years. Once again the goose-bumps came up on my arms as I realised that without any shadow of a doubt we had located Gino's family.

Emanuele said it was very emotional – even for him!

9

Ponte San Nicolo
In Memory of
Gino Marzotto

On Friday 12 April 2019 we set off to meet Lucia and
Angelina Marzotto in Ponte San Nicolo. These two ladies
were cousins, one the daughter of Gino and one the daughter
of his brother Antonio. Maybe they would invite us to their
home or maybe we would meet at the hotel where we were
staying. We only knew that Emanuele had made contact with
them and yes, they would like to meet us. They still had
photographs of my parent's visit in 1949 and Emanuele had
emailed them to me. I had shed a tear when I saw them as it
was so emotional. Here were people who knew my father
seventy-five years ago and still treasured the reminders they
had of him. Three years ago I never thought we would be able
to trace this family. I only knew they were a farming family in
Ponte San Nicolo with the eldest son named Gino. That was
all my mother could remember. Now with the magic of the
internet and social media Emanuele had miraculously found
me to ask for information on the POW camp in their town. He
was an historian from Ponte San Nicolo and then he took up
my challenge to find the Marzotto family and as they say, the
rest is history!

Once again we flew into Venice, collected our hire car and drove to Padua and the small town of Ponte San Nicolo. We drove along the main street again to show my sister the bridge from which the town gets its name. We even had supper at the same restaurant as the first time Brian and I had come to Ponte San Nicolo three years ago.

Emanuele and I exchanged text messages, me to say we had arrived safely and one from him saying he would come to our hotel at eleven o'clock the next morning.

He was a lovely young man and it was quickly decided that he would drive us around for the day in his car as he knew exactly where he was taking us. We were going to visit the old farmhouse first, as we were told the current owners had given permission for us to see it. It turned out to be several miles out into the countryside and to us would be described as a hamlet in the district of Ponte San Nicolo and not in the actual town of that name. As we arrived we could see that it was not in a habitable state but there were a lot of cars parked outside on the grass and we wondered what it was used for now as there were obviously people there. As we ventured up one side of this large building and turned the corner we were met by between eighty and ninety people all bunched together waiting to greet us. Angelina introduced herself and also Lucia and we hugged and kissed and cried. I asked if all the people were from the Marzotto family. Yes, all Marzotto family.

From the information I had from my father's letter to his parents, the one I call the Farmhouse Letter, he referred to Gino (married) Antonio (married) and Pasquina sister (unmarried at that time). What we didn't know was that there were a further seven sisters who had already married and left home so this family had comprised of eight daughters and two sons, ten siblings in total. Sadly, none of them are still living as they would be aged in the region of one hundred years old, but each of them had several children who seventy-five years later are now grandparents. It suddenly became clear that it was quite possible to have so many family members gathered together. In fact as the morning progressed we were aware that some of them had never met each other before. Our arrival had prompted such interest that it was like a family wedding. There were many who had never seen the farmhouse before either as it was where their grandparents had lived as children. No doubt often spoken about but now they had an opportunity to look around for themselves and it was a chance they didn't want to miss.

Guiseppe gave me a small photograph album and inside were all the pictures of us my father had sent them with his letters. One of his wedding day, one of him standing in the garden at home with his father, pictures of me and Fiona as babies, pictures of me as a five-year-old with my baby sister. It was overwhelmingly emotional to see that they were anticipating this visit as much as we were. It also confirmed my theory that my father must have sent pictures of his family including us, his two daughters, to his friends in Italy. I just knew he would have done. Guiseppe pointed to a picture of me as a toddler, digging a hole on the beach and then at me. 'You?'

'Yes me!' I laughed.

Fortunately there were a couple of the younger ones who could speak good English as we were shown inside the farmhouse. Martina was very helpful in translating for me and Fiona and also Daniel who had worked in London for many years paired up with Brian, so we were all able to understand what we were being shown. The farmhouse was built in the fifteenth century for monks who wove cloth on looms and so there was a chapel attached to one end of the building. It was a massive building by our standards and the rooms were huge. In a storage barn inside the same building we were shown a long row of huge barrels, each one would have had different contents like flour, wine, olive oil and so on. On the other side were pens for animals with a feeding trough along the wall. Apparently the trough once had wooden slatted sides which would have made it higher and on one occasion my father was hidden in this trough with the animal fodder and covered with straw. Another time he escaped through the house into the chapel and out into the countryside beyond. There was a hayloft with a big square hatch in one of the upstairs rooms. Sometimes my father had hidden up there to sleep, pulling the ladder up after himself and dropping a curtain down to cover the hole. They showed us the rooms where my parents slept when they came to visit in 1949 as an engaged couple. One room for all the women and one room for all the men.

Now that my sister has started to learn the Italian language, one of my mother's most famous memories of her visit can be explained. She asked the girls what they did all day and she thought that they told her they 'lingered in the khazi'. This was her little joke that she trotted out from time to time. We now realise that casalinga is actually the word for housewife!

We were told that in 1943 there had been a huge walnut tree outside the house. It had a hen coop high up in its branches and was another good hiding place where he spent many hours, once even hiding inside the hen coop at a particularly dangerous time. When he returned with my mother in 1949 he asked them 'Where is my tree?' He had hoped to show it to my mother. Sadly they had to tell him that it had died and they had to take it down. They said he cried. That tree must have represented a safe and secure place for him in times of dire distress.

So many little snippets were remembered and shared. So many photographs were taken. So many people who introduced themselves to us needed hugging and greeting. Gino's son Guiseppe who was six months old at the time my father wrote his letter about this family, told me who he was and I rocked my arms and said bambino! 'Si, Si'. I hope he was pleased that I had done my homework! It was Guiseppe who had given me the photograph album as slowly we learnt who was who. Now the time was getting on and lunch had been booked at a traditional restaurant near by. We had to go and there wasn't time for goodbyes, we were just whisked away.

We arrived at the restaurant to find many had followed us and a lunch was booked for seventy people. It was a lovely place and full of excited Italian chatter as we settled down to talk to the people seated around us. Opposite me was Lucia although I soon found out that everyone called her Bruna. No one seemed to know when or how it had started but Bruna was what she answered to. My sister thinks it is a nickname similar to the British calling a blonde girl 'Blondie' but for an Italian brunette. Her family had a bakery in Padua and at eighty-six years old she was still working there. She was a delightful lady with sparkling eyes and a cheeky smile and as old black and white photographs were produced by Angelina we could see that Lucia had been as glamorous as any pin-up girl when she was younger. Brian did a sterling job of putting names to everyone in the old photos. Even my mother, Patricia was in some of them. They must have been taken by my father and then sent to them later when the film had been developed. Of course as he was the photographer, he isn't in many of them but he does appear in a couple.

On my left was Martina who had been my guide and interpreter earlier at the farmhouse. She was a stunning twenty-one-year-old who stole my heart. Having had two sons and then two grandsons myself I teased that I would like to take her home with me as I had always wanted a daughter. She told me that she was an only child and I realised that she must be very special to her parents but later that evening I spoke with them and again teased that I would like to take her home with me and her mother said 'You can have her – for a year!' It was all in fun but maybe one day she will visit. Who knows! On my right was Elena who was married to Emanuele our original contact and the one who had planned and arranged this day for us. She also spoke good English and was aware of how much her husband had done to make this such a special day. I think they were quite anxious but they needn't have worried as everything was just perfect. We had a traditional Italian meal with risotto to start followed by slices of pork with sautéed potatoes and side dishes of hot spinach and cold grated carrot, grated onions, and grated red cabbage. Next was a delicious layered pastry with jam and cream.

At this point I decided the time was right to offer my English chocolates. There were seven tables of ten and opening the first box of Cadbury's Roses I went up and down the tables offering everyone a chocolate and a smile, hoping to make eye contact with everyone who had especially set aside today on their calendars to meet us. I soon had to open the second box and was glad I had brought three boxes with us. We had imagined maybe fifteen people would meet us so seventy was quite a stretch. I felt it was like the feeding of five thousand as I eked out one per person! The third box was opened as well. It was intended to be a gift to Emanuele and his wife but I hoped they understood my need to share it. (Once we were back home we posted them another box!)

Angelina stood up and went to stand in front of the tables and with a bit of hush called for, she started to read out a prepared speech. It was obviously a very emotional and heartfelt message and very difficult for her to deliver as she choked up several times so I got up and went and stood with my arm round her spurring her on and whispering: 'come on you can do this'. I don't suppose she knew what I was saying but I hoped the moral support helped. She gave the sheet of paper to me at the end saying the English translation was on the back. I read it out loud for the benefit of Brian and Fiona; some of the family seemed to think I had come with my own prepared speech!

She was thanking us The Ayers Ladies for making today possible and with Emanuele's help in arranging such a special day that she was able to visit the home where she had been born and spent her childhood. She was glad she could share this with her family and thanked the current owners for the opportunity. She wanted to marvel at the fact that there were still wonderful and compassionate people in the world despite the ugliness we so often see in the news. She ended with thank you, thank you, thank you.

The chatter resumed and people started to move about. So many lovely people came to say hello. Some had been to England and one couple had even had a holiday in Falmouth in the south west not so far from where we live. They had met in London where they worked in an Italian restaurant for several years before coming home to set up their own restaurant in Padua.

Eventually Emanuele explained that there was a meeting of his association that was taking place at six o'clock in the town later that evening and he hoped we would come too as he was giving a presentation. Brian, Fiona and I were taken back to our hotel for a break and a quick change of clothes but we had to be ready in just over an hour so there wasn't long to talk about what we had just experienced. We sat in the hotel reception area in shock and disbelief at what had just taken place and the number of people we had met, as Fiona said: 'We were just trying to process it all'.

We were back in reception at the appointed time to go to a meeting of 'about an hour' which would be conducted in their native Italian and we weren't quite sure what to expect but as Emanuele had done so much for us, it was the least we could do in the circumstances and we happily agreed. We parked and walked towards the hall. As I reached out to open the door I was aware of a promotional poster on the glass panel. There were two pictures of my mother and father and another picture of the farmhouse we had toured that same morning. A couple of sentences in Italian mentioned my name in bold lettering. I took a photo of it and started to realise that this meeting must have been arranged for some time and that it was about us and our father's story. We were led to the front row and introduced to Paola who would act as our interpreter. The room was already quite busy but it soon filled up and extra chairs were brought in. There were people standing everywhere and there were more people standing in the corridor outside. How many people were there? I don't know for sure but well over a hundred, maybe one hundred and fifty. It was a lot anyway.

Emanuele and another man gave their talks about the partisan movement and how the ordinary people of the countryside risked their lives to help the escaped prisoners of war. A representative of the Mayor said a few words as did other worthy people of the town. We were asked up to receive the gift of two books which were about Ponte San Nicolo. Then Guiseppe Marzotto the son of Gino, was asked to receive a plaque from the ANPI (Association Nationale of Partisans in Italy) which he was most honoured to receive in recognition of his father's courage and bravery in the war when he suffered brutal treatment at the hands of the fascists for being suspected of harbouring British prisoners, namely my father and his companion Victor; an accusation which Gino strenuously denied.

Next was the shock to be called up to receive a similar plaque, with a slightly stilted English translation of the same words.

Remembering the people who risked their lives
Refusing to bend heads in front of fascism
April 13th 2019

The microphone was passed to me. Would I like to say a few words? Yes of course I would, but what? I had not prepared for this. I had no speech ready in my pocket! First of all I apologised for not being able to speak Italian and that I would speak in English. That was fine as Paola had been brought up to the front to translate. I thanked everyone for coming. I thanked everyone for all that their families had done during the war to help British prisoners of war. They saved lives and we are forever grateful. My sister was keen to say a sentence that she had learnt in preparation for this trip and took the microphone from me. In a choked voice and in their native Italian she said: 'Without your family, our families would not exist'.

That was a perfect summing up for our unexpected moment in the spotlight. The meeting was over and we were asked to stand with the family to have pictures taken.

Everyone wanted to be in a photo with us. Everyone wanted to hug us. Some seemed happy to have just reached out and touched us. It was all slightly surreal to feel what it is like when the paparazzi descend on celebrities. The photographers here were mostly other family members, but there were a lot of them! Nobody wanted to break up the party atmosphere but when the caretaker switched off the lights for a few seconds we realised we had to move outside. As we hugged and said our goodbyes over and over again, they were saying 'ancora' 'ancora' which is 'again' 'again'.

That very special day will always be remembered as the day we met the Marzotto family. The date is etched on my commemorative plaque, a forever reminder that no matter how many years may pass, it is always possible to renew old friendships when the bond is so deep. I always knew that these people would feel like family to me. That if my father owed his life to them, I could trust them with mine.

They had pictures of me as a baby and as a toddler digging holes on the beach, it was as if they had known me all their life and in a way they had – I certainly felt I had known them all of mine.

10

Comunanza, 8 June 2019

Just eight weeks later Brian and I found ourselves in Italy once again. Since returning home from Ponte San Nicolo and the realization of a dream come true, we were invited to Comunanza on 8 June for a very special event taking place in the school.

The students there had won a national prize in a competition to celebrate individual acts of heroism both past and present. Their winning entry was a comic they had produced that told the story of the fisherman at Lampedusa who saved the lives of twelve drowning immigrants. The students had to travel to Milan to collect their prize and whilst there they were given seeds from the Garden of the Righteous in Jerusalem so that they could start their own garden in Comunanza. These Gardens of the Righteous appear all over the world and it was a huge honour for the school and the village to be given this status. 8 June was set as the date for the grand occasion and I was asked if I would like to attend as they would be honouring the family Cozzi who looked after my father and hid him from the Germans. Although we did not quite understand everything that was going to happen that day, I felt it was important enough to attend especially as they had invited us. So, in less than two weeks we arranged our diaries and booked flights and were in Italy once again.

It was starting to feel like our second home. It was warm and sunny as we set off from the airport to drive to Comunanza. We travelled the day before the event and arrived at our now familiar hotel to be greeted by Peppe in the traditional Italian way. Fiametta was our family link and translator and joined us for dinner so that we could go over the plans for the following day. There was to be an event in the Town Hall which would begin with some music played by the students. This was to be followed by various presentations and speeches and if I was willing, they wanted to ask me six prepared questions; her brother Emilio was in the class that had produced the comic and won the competition. The students would translate the questions and my answers to the audience; in this way they could combine their history project with comprehension and spoken English.

These amazing fourteen-year-olds were in their final year of Middle School. At this stage students go on to a specialist High School of their choice and Fiametta had gone to a Languages School; she was now nineteen and about to start university in Rome the following September. In Italy, students attend school on Saturday mornings and on this particular Saturday, 8th June it was their last day of term. This meant that Fiametta was unable to attend the special event in Comunanza because her own class in Ascoli were having end of term celebrations, especially poignant because they would be splitting up to go their separate ways. However, she prepared me well and promised that Alessia, her mother's friend would be on hand to do the translations as she had the very first time we came to Comunanza. Fiametta's mother Patrizia and Alessia would both collect us in the morning. The school and the Town Hall were situated just behind the hotel but we were driven right up to the building and introduced to the Mayor and his wife, to

Francesco the journalist who had written up our story on our very first visit and who was to be the MC on this occasion. To the teachers who had been involved with the project and to the President of the local Lions Club. Added to this were many of the Cozzi family who were now old friends and welcome familiar faces in a crowd of so many strangers. Eventually we were ushered in and took our reserved seats near the front.

The Town Hall was comfortably furnished with tiered upholstered seating and packed with students, parents, friends and supporters. The stage was filling up with students, guitarists seated at the front and recorder players filling up the rest. The front of the stage had been decorated by Patrizia with elaborate festoons of evergreen fir branches with white ribbons symbolizing writing paper. The first section of the event was a musical rendition of three tunes related to the topic. The first was John Lennon's 'Imagine', the second one was not familiar to me, but I recognized the third piece as 'Joy to the World'. This was followed by a Power Point presentation of various hero's like Schindler, with wartime images such as the gates of Auschwitz. After this the dignitaries congratulated the staff and pupils for all their hard work in winning the competition but especially for getting this special recognition for Comunanza. Every guest speaker was given a copy of the winning comic and if it was a lady they also received a beautiful long-stemmed white rose wrapped in white lace. This included the teachers who had been congratulated on their efforts. The stage was eventually cleared and a curved row of seats placed in readiness for the next part; Alessia whispered to me: 'I think this is your turn now'.

I was invited up and seated in the middle with students from the class who had won the competition. Their teacher sat beside me to translate, but it was unnecessary as one of the students was exceptionally good at English and thought she could manage the job and manage she did! She was able to listen to me speak for three or four minutes when I would pause at a natural break for her to translate and repeat to the audience and her fellow students what I had just said. I was asked my questions in English by each of the six questioners and this was translated as well. It was quite a laborious process but an impressive display of their knowledge of the English language at fourteen years of age.

Then Elisa and Maria Cozzi, the two cousins that I had first met three years earlier and who are some of the last living links I have with my father were tenderly helped up to the stage. Elisa was amazing. She spoke with passion about a visit by the senior German Officers in the region at the time my father was there in hiding. He had managed to get up the hillside into a hidden cave whilst the Germans took over the house for the day. She remembered a duck had been killed and roasted to make a stew and that the family were most hospitable as they did not want to appear put out or anxious in the face of this intrusion. I do not know everything she said but the teacher beside me was most helpful in giving me a brief summing up.

The students had experienced a unique real life insight into the past history of their village and together with the Garden that was about to be blessed by the local Priest and inaugurated by the Mayor I would hope it was a day that none of them will ever forget.

We left the Town Hall and drove to the neighboring school building where it was now midday and the sun was at its highest. Outside we gathered for photographs and awaited the moment the sign would be unveiled. The Priest held a short service and then I was led away to watch while two students planted the seeds that had come from Jerusalem. The ceremonials were now over and we could go into the school for refreshments and shade. The central table was groaning under a mountain of finger buffet type food. There were local delicacies and an incredible ball shaped loaf that was sliced, made into sandwiches, re-assembled and cut through in quarters. Each layer of sandwich had a different filling and as people took a piece to eat, the cross section of this sphere was revealed like strata of rock in all its different colours. We chatted with many people including another journalist who incidentally was a mother of two children at the school and worked with Francesco; also many more family members from the Cozzi family who I tried to place on the family tree in my head but struggled. I don't even know all the names of my aunt's grandchildren and great-grandchildren who are in Australia and I have never met, but hard as it is, I still try to make the connections between cousins, nieces and nephews of a family in Italy that I only met three years ago. It is strange but I feel I owe them the respect of remembering each and every one of them and it has become my way to return the love and affection showered on me.

We were invited to a family birthday party that evening. The birthday boy was called Brando and he was two! We were to be collected at half past eight and we imagined this was just an excuse for an adult's party and that Brando would be in bed. Boy were we wrong there! This was Italy! Brando and his five-year-old sister Leticia were wide awake and still partying when we said our goodbyes three hours later.

Fiametta also had plans to take us out earlier that afternoon once she was home from her last day at college, so we had a quick siesta for an hour and were then whisked away to the beautiful village of Amandola where we had a fabulous ice-cream with one of the teachers from the school. She was there waiting for us with her daughter and a cute dog. Her husband was the chef and our ice-creams were in huge sundae glasses and covered in whipped cream. Delicious but we were defeated by the end!

The girls suggested we do a tour of this picturesque village and we readily agreed. Little did we know it was all uphill with glimpses of the surrounding countryside though gaps in the houses. Those gaps were the perfect excuse to stop and take some photographs whilst catching our breath before the next section!

Eventually we reached the top and were rewarded with seats around a children's play area. The others were talking to a man who turned out to be the proprietor of a small boutique hotel in this top of the world place. He used to have a hotel close by with forty bedrooms, but it had been damaged in the earthquakes and he had been forced to close it. He moved next door to his father's old house where he had spent the last three years renovating it and although it only had six bedrooms, he was proud to show us around.

After that, it didn't seem to take very long to get back down to the car parked in the square below and after saying our goodbyes we were driven off by Fiametta to visit the old farmhouse where Elisa and Leo had lived until ill-health and old age had forced them to move into a modern flat in the village. We were told it was very similar to the one the Cozzi family had lived in when my father found a safe haven there in 1943. It was sadly deserted and in need of renovation but was a great example of a traditional old farmhouse.

We were returned to our hotel once again and had a few hours to rest from the unaccustomed heat, to send messages home and to review the photos we had taken.

Now in the third change of clothes that day we were collected by Federica and her boyfriend to go to the birthday party. Brando's grandparents hosted the party. Having been made homeless three years ago after the earthquake in Norcia they had found an industrial unit in Comunanza to live in, which they had converted into a home. We were invited into a large out of doors room attached to their unit. It had three sides and a ceiling, but the fourth side just had a low picket fence and gate, but the room was open and airy. The gates were especially necessary for the safety of the small children, as beyond the unit was an open car park.

We were once again treated to the local party food with homemade crispy pizza slices, melon and ham, and the local speciality of the Ascoli Region, breaded and deep-fried balls of olives stuffed with meat. There was local bread, pastries and plenty to drink. That weekend I discovered a liking of sparkling water, something I had always said I disliked, so not being a big fan of alcohol, I was happy to drink the Aqua Frizzante.

This strand of the family was Maria's and there were about twenty people there. Maria was one of the two older ladies that I had first met and who remembered my father in 1943. She and her husband Quinto had two childen; Tonino (married to Roberta) and Anna-Rita (married to Corrado). Tonino had three daughters and Anna-Rita a daughter and a son. Of the three daughters of Tonino, Laura the eldest was the mother of the birthday boy Brando and his sister Leticia. Federica was the middle daughter and our personal host and translator. Having worked for a year in Poland, she explained that English was the common language there, so she was an excellent interpreter for us that evening. The youngest of the three was Aurora.

Anna-Rita's two children were more familiar to us as they had appeared at the very first meeting and it was her daughter Alessia who had suggested we use Facebook as a way of communicating and I am forever grateful, as this has proved to be a very useful tool as it offers a translation of anything written in a foreign language. Her son Andrea was in the class that won the competition along with Fiametta's brother Emilio. Amazingly to us he was leaving around ten o'clock to drive to see his girlfriend. This fourteen-year-old was very happy to show off his vehicle that was a small car powered by a very small engine, but much safer than any moped. He belted himself in and started up the engine and it sounded similar to a lawnmower but none the less it was his first taste of independence. I asked his mother if he had a job to pay for it and she replied: 'No, but I do!' Little had we known that as we drove around the streets of Italy there were fourteen-year-olds alongside us! We presume there must have been some sort of proficiency test, but it didn't cross our minds to ask as we were so stunned by this strange phenomenon.

We finally said our goodbyes to this family group at a quarter to midnight worried that Peppe would be waiting up for us at the hotel. What a day it had been. It seemed impossible that we had crammed so much into a single day.

The following morning Fiametta had promised to come to the hotel to say goodbye before we set off on our journey to the airport. She asked if we would like to go and visit Elisa and Leo in their flat just behind the hotel and we were delighted to have the chance to see them again. I had seen Elisa at the school the previous day, but it was a brief hug and no time to properly communicate with her. Leo had not been at the celebrations as his health had deteriorated and he now needed to be on oxygen. Elisa seemed to have recovered from her brain operation of three years ago but they were both very frail and the half an hour or so we spent with them was very special. She had lost her daughter Aida to cancer since our last visit. Aida had been my friend and buddy from our first encounter with this family in 2016. When I first met her, I didn't catch her name, but she said 'Aida, like the opera.' I got it then and never forgot it. We became Facebook Friends sending messages at birthdays and Christmas. She was the chief organiser of the family. Everyone seemed to know and love her. She was a one off and it had been a sudden death as she had been given a cautious but optimistic all-clear only a month earlier. Fiametta had taken us to the cemetery the day before and I took my white long-stemmed rose and planted it in a flowerpot at her grave. I was telling Elisa this, but she knew already, 'Si, Si'. It transpired she had taken hers too and placed it next to mine.

In Comunanza all of the descendants of the Cozzi family and in Ponte San Nicolo all the members of the Marzotto family have made us feel so very welcome. The way they have embraced us into their families and included us in everything is beyond my comprehension. It is as if there is no language barrier or gap of over seventy years but instead a lifelong friendship that was always there but is just being resumed as if the in-between years had never happened.

My sister has started to learn the language with a real passion, what greater incentive could she have? I have surprised myself by the passion I have for writing and recording our remarkable story. Who would ever have thought that a few days holiday taken in 2016 to drive the route my father had walked in 1943 would take us to a point where three years later not only have I been able to find the two lost families in Italy that helped to save my father's life but in

both villages, the families have now been publicly acknowl-
edged for the heroic actions of their parents.

I am proud to have been a catalyst for all that has taken
place since 2016 and I hope my father would be proud to see
what has been achieved in his name which lives on as **_Luigi_**.

Epilogue

I have come to the end of a journey which has revealed so much more to us than we ever imagined possible when we set out in 2016. A simple trip to Italy to drive the route my father walked in the war has had an incredible domino effect as one thing led to another. First we found one of the two families he corresponded with after the war, more by luck than judgement. Then a newspaper story followed this chance reunion and nearly two years later, because of that article, Emanuele, a historian from Ponte San Nicolo, contacted me about the Prisoner of War Camp in his town. With the added discovery of my father's letters and the details I had since found of the family in Ponte San Nicolo, Emanuele managed to find them for me, something I never thought possible.

In 1949, after the war was over, my father had returned with his then fiancée to introduce her to these two farming families that had saved his life. My mother often referred to 'the Italians' and although I was only six when my father died I had grown up with an inbuilt sense of knowing that these families were part of my history and were out there somewhere.

In April 2019 we eagerly looked forward to seeing the family in Ponte San Nicolo. This was the final piece of the puzzle but in many ways the most important. They gave my father refuge in his first six weeks of liberty, telling him he was like a son to them. They helped him to evade capture with Gino suffering physical brutality. All this adds up to heroism of the first order. It was another tearful reunion but one that I relished. They were no longer strangers to me but family.

Back in November 2017 when my sister and I discovered my father's letters, the letters which gave me a focus and a project in my first year of retirement I had no idea what it would lead to. This book tells the story of my quest to find the two families in Italy who gave my father sanctuary and friendship. It has meant a great deal to me to be able to explain why my father had never answered their letters or returned to see them. To meet these people and thank them for all the sacrifices they and their parents made during the war. At last, in his place, I have made this connection and given them the explanation they deserve.

Had he lived we imagine we would have spent many happy holidays in Italy. He would have wanted us to meet these wonderful people, to know them as he did and to visit the places he wrote about. As I write in 2019, it is eighty years since the start of World War Two and what better time to share this intensely heart-warming story that is in itself a new chapter of our family history.

We are looking forward to another reunion in March 2020 when our children and grandchildren will meet the family in Ponte San Nicolo and the next generation becomes part of this amazing story.

Unfortunately this visit had to be cancelled due to the Coronavirus pandemic.

However my hope is that it will happen one day soon.

Lightning Source UK Ltd.
Milton Keynes UK
UKHW020753051121
393425UK00006B/133

9 781839 750908